To Tom.
Keep the faith.

[signature]
12.91

Book I

CHRISTIAN SERPAS

Acadian House
PUBLISHING
LAFAYETTE, LOUISIANA

ABOUT THE COVER: Tom Dempsey kicks the longest field goal in National Football League history, 63 yards, on November 8, 1970, to beat the Detroit Lions, 19-17. The holder was Joe Scarpati.

-- Illustration by Tony O. Champagne,
  New Orleans, Louisiana

ABOUT THIS BOOK...
"The New Orleans Saints: 25 Years of Heroic Effort (Book I)" is the first of a two-book set commemorating the 25-year history of the New Orleans Saints. It deals with the ups and downs of the Saints from their inception in 1967 through their first winning season, in 1987. Book II, scheduled for publication in March of 1992, covers the 1988 thru 1991 seasons, when the Saints were built into a championship-calibre team, under the direction of Coach Jim Mora and General Manager Jim Finks.

© Copyright 1991 by Acadian House
Publishing, Inc.

All rights reserved, including the right to reproduce this book or portions thereof in any form whatsoever. For information, contact Acadian House Publishing, P.O. Box 52247, Lafayette, Louisiana 70505.

Published by:
ACADIAN HOUSE PUBLISHING
Lafayette, Louisiana

ISBN: 0-925417-09-2

Printed in the United States of America
by Walsworth Press, Marceline, Missouri

Preface

It was so loud I couldn't hear myself think, as the chants of "Go Saints Go" bombarded my senses and took precedence over everything else in the immediate vicinity. Bobby Hebert had just thrown his second touchdown pass of the brand-new 1988 regular season, and the Saints were on top of the eventual Super Bowl champion 49ers, 14-7.

I had seen these types of spontaneous celebrations many times throughout Saints history, in Tulane Stadium, the Louisiana Superdome, even, on a much smaller scale, in our family living room.

But what made this emotional explosion unique was that I wasn't witnessing it in any of those familiar settings. I wasn't even in Louisiana. I was living in California at the time and watching the game in a little sports bar in Marina Del Ray called Sports Harbor.

But the same electricity that was lighting up the Dome and countless living rooms and watering holes along the bayous back home was also charging this gathering clear across the country. As I looked around the room at the horde of New Orleans expatriates who packed the Harbor every time the Saints played, I realized that although they had left Louisiana, they'd taken their Saints with them.

That night I began writing this book.

Contrary to what a lot of people may think, the Saints' initial winning season in 1987 didn't cap 20 years of barren wasteland. During those two decades the Saints had their share of triumphs along with the disappointments: John Gilliam's return of the opening kickoff in the Saints' first league game, Billy Kilmer's six touchdown passes in one game, Tom Dempsey's NFL record 63-yard field goal, the arrival of Archie Manning, the explosiveness of Hank Stram's "Thunder and Lightning" backfield, and the top-rated defense of the Bum Phillips Era. And the years were full of heroes like Dave Whitsell, Doug Atkins, Danny Abramowicz, George Rogers, Hokie Gajan and Morten Andersen, to name but a few.

But even while in the midst of seemingly endless losses,

the Saints have consistently been one of the most colorful stories in the NFL, perhaps most dramatically demonstrated by the "Baghead Saga" during the 1980 1-win, 15-loss disaster.

Researching the historical facts and figures for a book can often become tedious and even boring. Not so with this project. In fact, the line was often blurred between research fact-finding and enjoyable entertainment. I was also helped by the fact that a good portion of the material I needed was waiting in my own files. Since the Saints' inception, especially in their early years, I had saved books, magazines and newspaper clippings dealing with the Saints and with football in general. And when much of the 20 years of accumulated information was used in this book, I was finally able to decisively answer my own eternal question, "What am I saving all this stuff for?"

I tried to write the book that I, as a sports fan, would want to read, a book of events, not of statistics, full of human interest stories, with just enough stats to illustrate the points being made in the chapters. I trust that this format will make for enjoyable reading.

-- CHRISTIAN SERPAS
New Orleans, 1991

About the Author

Veteran sports writer CHRISTIAN SERPAS was born in New Orleans and grew up in adjacent St. Bernard Parish, where he has resided for most of his life.

At the age of 15 he interviewed both the Pittsburgh Steelers and Minnesota Vikings, combatants in Super Bowl IX, which resulted in his first published newspaper article, in the *St. Bernard News*. Since then, his feature stories have been published in a number of newspapers and magazines, including a series of articles on the history of professional football.

In 1985 he co-hosted a local television show, "TV Open House," with his father, Paul F. Serpas. In 1990 he wrote and hosted a regularly scheduled New Orleans radio show titled "Saints Snapshots," which became a popular feature among Saints fans.

Photo Credits

Erby Aucoin, New Orleans, La., 9, 10, 15, 18, 23, 25, 34, 37, 39, 43, 46;
Brad Kemp, *The Daily Advertiser*, 89, 99, 105;
Guy Reynolds, *The Morning Advocate*, 101, 109;
Bill Feig, *The Morning Advocate*, 13, 71, 87, 95;
Stephan Savoia, *The Morning Advocate*, 110;
Charles Gerald, *The Morning Advocate*, 63;

Acknowledgements

The author would like to thank some people whose cooperation made the task of writing about a quarter of a century of football games a little less daunting.

Anne Perez in the Saints Media Relations office, whose generosity and willingness to make historical data available to me was extremely helpful. Ken Trahan of the Saints Hall of Fame Museum, who opened his doors for me on countless occasions. Saints play-by-play broadcaster Larry Matson, for his assistance during the time I was doing my "Saints Snapshots" radio show. (He was the station's sports director at the time.)

For the photographs, I thank Mona Hatfield and Mark Keedy at the Baton Rouge *Morning Advocate*; Bruce Brown, sports editor of the Lafayette *Daily Advertiser*; and Erby Aucoin, the Saints' director of photography for 19 years before his retirement in 1986, who made his photo files available to me.

I'd also like to thank Joe Chambers, editor of the *St. Bernard News*, who gave me my first professional sports writing assignment; my wife, Melissa, the biggest Saints fan I've ever known, for putting up with the lights on all night in the writing room and the rattling of the typewriter; my sister, Mary, for her encouragement; and Johnny Indovina for his enthusiasm toward the project.

Finally, I wish to thank the staff of Acadian House Publishing and its manager, Trent Angers, for perceiving the value of this book and for working tirelessly to bring it to fruition in record time. -- C.S.

Dedication

This book is dedicated to my parents -- to my mother, Helen G. Serpas, who through the years has encouraged me to concentrate on writing, and to my father, Paul F. Serpas, the finest man I've ever known, and one of the top two writers in my family. -- C.S.

Table of Contents

1. The Saints Come Marching In 11
2. Blastoff! 14
3. The 'Weasel' And The 'Flea' 19
   (Dave Whitsell & Walt Roberts)
4. 'Ol' Whiskey' (Billy Kilmer) 21
5. Every Boy's Hero (Danny Abramowicz) 31
6. Old Warriors, New Battlefield 35
   (Jim Taylor & Doug Atkins)
7. When Hats Were Black 38
8. 'Thunderfoot' (Tom Dempsey) 41
9. Archie Is A Saint (Archie Manning) 45
10. Black Sunday 49
11. Squeezing 'The Juice' 51
12. A Victory For The Crowd 54
13. The Hank Stram Era 57
14. Archie On Ice 62
15. 'Thunder and Lightning' 65
    (Tony Galbreath & Chuck Muncie)
16. SuperManning 70
17. 'Big Ben' 75
18. The Falcons Strike Again 77
19. Snakebit (Ken Stabler) 80
20. The Baghead Saga 82
21. Faith, Hope And 'Bum' 85
    (Bum Phillips)
22. 'King George' (George Rogers) 88
23. Heartbreaker 91
24. Hokie (Hokie Gajan) 93
25. No Mora Excuses (Jim Mora) 98
26. Johnny Comes Marching Home 100
    (John Fourcade)
27. The Promised Land 108

The New Orleans SAINTS
25 Years Of Heroic Effort

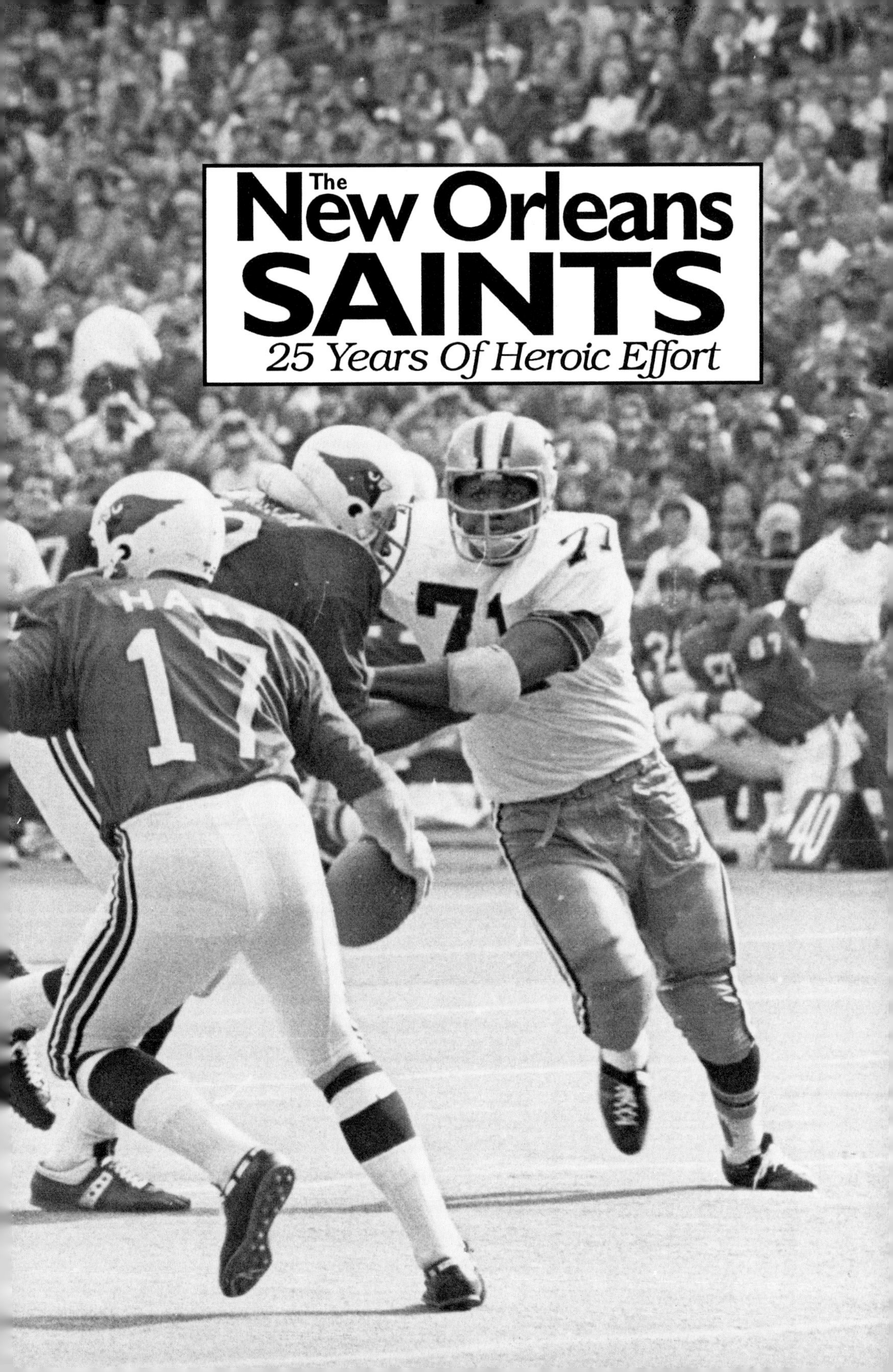

Tulane Stadium, 1967

The Saints Come Marching In

1967

New Orleans businessman Dave Dixon had a vision: To base a pro football team in the city and build a domed stadium for them to play in. For five years, beginning in 1961, Dixon and his associates tried to bring pro football to town. In 1963 they were ready to buy the Oakland Raiders and move them to New Orleans, but the deal fell through when they couldn't meet the $400,000 price tag. Still, Dixon's group persisted, and finally, on All Saints Day 1966, New Orleans was granted a National Football League franchise by commissioner Pete Rozelle.

The price of the franchise was $8 million, and in December of 1966 John Mecom Jr. became the owner and president.

A contest was then held to name the new team, but it was really no contest at all. There was little doubt all along that the team would take its name from the classic song "When the Saints Go Marching In." And on January 9, 1967, the sixteenth member of the NFL was officially christened "The Saints."

The merchandising bonanza which hit New Orleans with the Saints' arrival was unprecedented in NFL history. Two major department stores, D. H. Holmes and Maison Blanche, were authorized as Saints Pro Shops, and both were swamped. Holmes reported doing twice the volume they had done in Atlanta when the Falcons were born; by season's end they had reordered some items more than a dozen times.

Anything with a Saints emblem on it sold--decals, pennants, pajamas, radios, tie clasps, big lamps with a Saints helmet as a base and even Saints luggage. But possibly the biggest seller of all was the Saints "bobbing head" doll. Tens of thousands of these wide-eyed, smiling mascots were sold at a dollar apiece, with one store selling 200 dozen in the first ten days.

It was obvious that the Saints had fans. Now they needed players. To assure New Orleans a nucleus of veteran talent, a special expansion draft was held. The Saints were allowed to select three unprotected players from each of the other NFL teams, excluding Atlanta. From this talent pool the Saints picked men such as Steve Stonebreaker, Dave Whitsell, Walt "Flea" Roberts, Joe Wendryhoski, Jake Kupp, Paul Hornung and Billy Kilmer.

The Saints also used trades to collect more veterans like Doug Atkins, Gary Cuozzo, Ernie Wheelwright, and former Louisiana State University great Jim Taylor.

In the college draft, the Saints made Alabama fullback Les Kelley their first ever pick. They also drafted John Gilliam, Bo Burris, Del Williams, Dave Rowe, Don McCall and in the seventeenth and final round, a flanker named Danny Abramowicz.

The games were now approaching, and when season tickets went on sale, the Saints sold an NFL record 20,000 on the

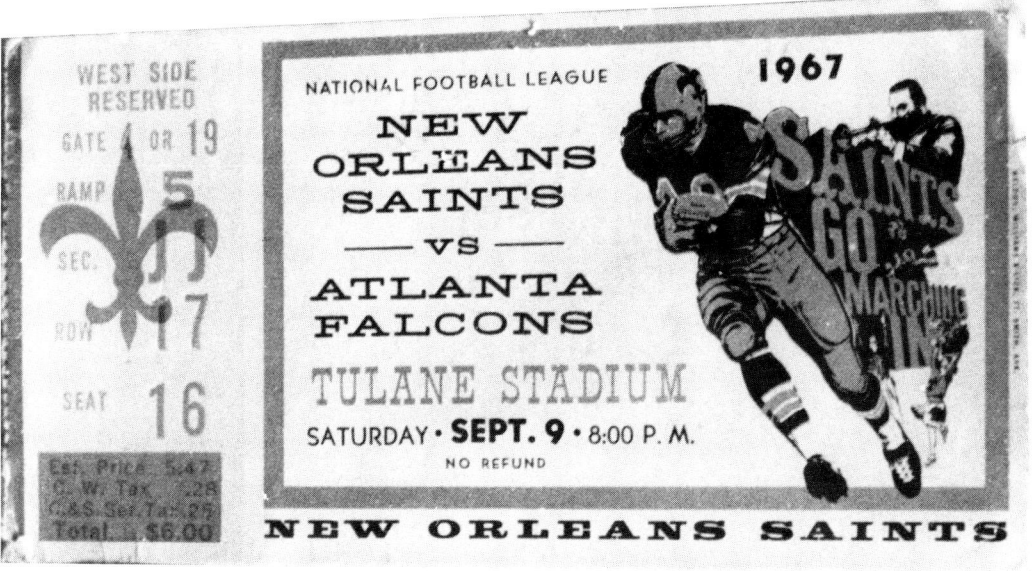

A ticket for the Saints' first ever home game, a pre-season meeting with the Atlanta Falcons, on Saturday, September 9, 1967 in Tulane Stadium. The Saints won, 27-14, before 67,486 fans.

first day. Eventually, 33,400 were sold before the first league game kicked off.

As expected, The Saints lost their first NFL pre-season contest to the Rams, 16-7 in Anaheim Stadium. But the next week, infant New Orleans beat the St. Louis Cardinals in Shreveport, and followed that surprise by defeating Pittsburgh in Baton Rouge. They then added road victories over both San Francisco and Miami before returning home for their New Orleans debut. More than 67,000 screaming fans turned out to watch the Saints dump Atlanta 27-14, completing a 5-1 preseason mark, and setting another NFL expansion team record.

As the crowd cheered and sang under the huge fireworks display that lit up the night sky over old Tulane Stadium for the first Saints home game, surely Dave Dixon and his group were proud to be in that number -- when New Orleans, finally, went marching in, to the NFL.

Blastoff

September 17, 1967

At 1:35 p.m. on Sunday, September 17, 1967 a little-known New Orleans Saints rookie running back named John Gilliam received the opening kickoff of the Saints' first official NFL game. Fifteen seconds later Gilliam was famous, as the Saints entered the NFL in the most dramatic fashion in league history.

Nearly 81,000 rabid Saints fans had shown up for the inaugural festivities surrounding the opening day game with the Los Angeles Rams. They stomped and cheered, danced and hollered throughout the pre-game entertainment, player introductions and National Anthem. But as the crowd stood on their feet and watched the opening kickoff from the Rams' Bruce Gossett sail toward the Saints' return men -- veteran Walt "Flea" Roberts and rookie John Rally Gilliam -- no one, especially Gilliam, could have realistically anticipated the events of the next few seconds. But those next few seconds would forever cement Gilliam's place in Saints and NFL history.

John Gilliam, shown here reaching for an over-thrown pass, is the player who returned the opening kickoff of the Saints' first game 94 yards for a touchdown.

"I was a rookie, nervous and afraid. The football was kicked down the middle, and I prayed to the Lord, 'Please go to the Flea.' But Roberts called it for me. I caught it and took off running to save my hide. I ran behind a wedge of blockers and went past them about midfield. I veered to my left, and I was running free. What a great feeling. What a super feeling!" Gilliam recalls.

Ninety-four yards later Gilliam crossed the Rams' goal line and threw the ball over the end zone hedges into the roaring, swarming crowd, as the old steel rafters of Tulane Stadium shook under the rolling celebration. The crowd noise was deafening, and the seismograph at nearby Loyola University registered at 32, indicating something akin to an earthquake. As the other Saints mobbed Gilliam in the end zone, thousands of shirt-sleeved, shell-shocked Saints fans laughed and danced, hoarsely shouting along as the Saints band blasted "When the Saints Go Marching In."

On the first play, of the first game, of their first season, the Saints had scored a touchdown. Even the Saints themselves were impressed.

Bill Kilmer, Saints quarterback, remembers it well: "I was on the sidelines waiting to go in for the first play when Gilliam just took off, had a big hole and went right through it. After winning our last five exhibition games, the last one against Atlanta, we had the whole town rocking. Gilliam's run was the culmination."

Steve Stonebreaker, Saints linebacker: "I was on the sidelines trying to get the thunder of the crowd out of my ears from the ovation to Jimmy Taylor when he was the last player introduced. The roar that greeted him was unbelievable and unforgettable. Then came Gilliam's flight. That was a miracle."

Tom Fears, Saints head coach, and former All Pro player with the Rams: "What a dream start for a new franchise, and especially against the Rams. This was my first head coaching job, something I'd worked for all my life. I wish that moment could have lasted forever."

Of course, it didn't, but that didn't matter. It also didn't matter that the Saints were pulled back down to earth as the Rams eventually won, 27-13. What did matter was that the moment had happened, and the Saints had arrived in unprecedented style.

But John Gilliam, the man who delivered the Saints' arrival

message to the NFL, almost didn't arrive in New Orleans himself. Gilliam was a track star in high school, and only tried out for football in his senior year to prove his courage to his classmates. He became the team's most valuable player, receiving several scholarship offers, and choosing South Carolina State, where he was an All Conference selection for three years at three different positions, end, flanker and halfback.

Gilliam made the most of his opportunity the first time he touched the ball for the Saints, and throughout the 1967 and '68 seasons he was used as a return specialist, in addition to his regular duties as flanker. Early in the 1967 season, following his amazing opening day return, Gilliam was even used in the regular running back rotation.

Following the 1968 season, Gilliam was traded to St. Louis, and in 1972 he moved on to Minnesota. There he enjoyed his greatest success, helping the Vikings to two National Football Conference (NFC) titles and appearances in Super Bowls VIII and IX. In 1975, lured by a massive salary, Gilliam was one of the big NFL stars to jump to the new World Football League, playing with the Chicago Winds. But when the rival league folded he finished out the '75 season with the Vikings. He spent 1976 with the Atlanta Falcons before, fittingly, returning to the Saints to finish out his career in 1977 in the Superdome.

"I was traded, but I never lost my love for the Saints. I will always be a Saint. I have pictures of the run on my living room wall to remind me of it. John Mecom sent them to me," Gilliam says.

John Gilliam ended his career as he began it, in a New Orleans Saints uniform. He was the spark that lit the fuse for the first Saints fan explosion. By the end of the 1967 opening day game with Los Angeles, 15 spectators had been taken out on stretchers, and Rams players were referring to Tulane Stadium as "Bedlam Bowl." By the end of the 1967 season, New Orleans had set an NFL first-year attendance record, averaging more than 75,000 fans per game.

With Gilliam's opening touchdown return, the Saints were off and running.

Dave "The Weasel" Whitsell blocks a punt, scoops it up, and returns it 16 yards for a score during a Saints' victory over the Redskins in 1968.

The 'Weasel' And The 'Flea'

November 5, 1967

The year was 1967. Despite a promising 5-1 pre-season mark, New Orleans had been getting a rough initiation to the NFL fraternity. Halfway through their inaugural 14-game schedule, the Saints remained winless.

The team that represented New Orleans that first year in the NFL was an odd mixture of battle-tested veterans like Doug Atkins, other teams' castoffs like Billy Kilmer, and unknown rookies like Danny Abramowicz.

Walt Roberts and Dave Whitsell both came to the Saints through the expansion draft, as other teams' castoffs. Roberts, also known as "Flea," was a fourth-year split end who wasn't drafted by the pros, but who had played three years with the Cleveland Browns. Whitsell, a cornerback known as the "Weasel," was in his tenth year after playing three with the Detroit Lions and six with the Chicago Bears, including their

1963 NFL championship season.

Both men were considered expendable by their former teams, but both were considered very valuable by Saints coach Tom Fears. And on Sunday, November 5, 1967, these two men sparked the Saints to their first NFL victory, a 31-24 thriller over the Philadelphia Eagles.

Tulane Stadium's smallest crowd of the year, less than 60,000, were still taking their seats when Roberts took the opening kickoff back 91 yards for a touchdown. On the first play of the second quarter, Roberts picked up teammate Jim Taylor's fumble and raced 28 yards for another six. When the Eagles pulled to within seven points, Whitsell stepped in. The Weasel snatched a Norm Snead pass and returned his seventh interception of the year 41 yards for a score. In the fourth quarter, the Flea closed out his record three-touchdown day by pulling in a 49-yard bomb from quarterback Gary Cuozzo. Whitsell and the defense then held off the Eagles' aerial assault, and New Orleans had its first NFL win, 31-24.

For their efforts, both Roberts and Whitsell were named NFL Back of the Week. Roberts finished the season with five touchdowns and led the Saints in punt returns. He was traded to Detroit after the '67 season and finished out his career with Washington in 1970.

Whitsell ended with a league-leading 10 interceptions, returned two for touchdowns, and was named United Press International's Comeback Player of the Year. He also blocked three field goals and two extra points and became the first Saint ever named to the Pro Bowl. He returned to the Saints for two more seasons after 1967 and that historic win -- when the Flea and the Weasel fleeced the Eagles.

'Ol' Whiskey'

Billy Kilmer 1967 - 1970

Billy Kilmer was the last of a breed, the final installment of a book that included chapters on such legendary characters as Bobby Layne, Sid Luckman, Y.A. Tittle, and Norm Van Brocklin. As he hoarsely shouted the signals from behind his single-bar facemask, chinstrap hanging unbuckled, socks drooping down low around his ankles, Kilmer was a throwback to another era. It was an era when quarterbacks not only ran and passed for wins, but occasionally willed their teammates to victory.

"If Kilmer climbed up atop a building and jumped off, I believe the other guys would follow. He's that kind of leader, the same kind as Bobby Layne," says Dave Whitsell, one of Kilmer's teammates.

For the first four years of the franchise's history, 6 foot, 204 pound Billy Kilmer was the New Orleans Saints quarterback, but mostly, he was their leader. More than any other player of the era, Kilmer symbolized the early, rollicking

Saints. On an expansion team made up mostly of other teams' castoffs and league misfits, "Ol' Whiskey's" two-fisted, hard-living, lead-by-example type of personality fit like a glove.

As a teammate later on in his career would say, "He's the toughest guy I've ever seen. How can anybody even think of quitting when he's leading your team."

Kilmer himself had never thought of quitting along the tough road that led him to New Orleans in 1967. Following a sparkling collegiate career at UCLA, where he led the nation in total offense in his All-American senior season, Kilmer, who also played basketball for the Bruins, was the number one draft choice of the 49ers in 1961. As a tailback, Kilmer was the triggerman for San Francisco's explosive shotgun offense in 1962, but with two games left in the season, on the way home from a hunting trip, Kilmer fell asleep at the wheel of his '57 Chevy and crashed into a roadside ditch. His right leg was broken at the ankle and he laid unconscious and partially submerged in the stagnant water for more than an hour. The doctors' predictions were gloomy: most probably death, or at best, life with a permanent limp, and definitely without football.

But Kilmer didn't think of quitting. Even when an infection caused by the stagnant water threatened amputation, he didn't even entertain the thought.

"When you think negatively, that's what starts pulling you down. I've never accepted injuries as something that's going to stop me. You've got to fight 'em. The way I look at an injury, it's just a little roadblock that you fight," Kilmer reasoned.

Kilmer didn't play in the 1963 season, but by 1964 he was well enough to see limited action. He then missed all of the '65 schedule and only played briefly in '66 before the 49ers made him available to the Saints in the expansion draft of 1967.

Due to his lack of true quarterbacking experience, Kilmer came into New Orleans second on the quarterback depth chart behind Gary Wood, who had proven himself a capable signal-caller in relief situations as a New York Giant. But before the college draft in mid-March, the Saints traded their number one

Billy Kilmer (center) talks strategy with head coach Tom Fears and receiver John Gilliam during a 38-21 loss to the Giants in Yankee Stadium in 1968. Kilmer overcame tremendous odds, recovering from a near-fatal auto accident in 1962, to become the fiery leader of the early Saints.

choice to Baltimore for quarterback Gary Cuozzo, Johnny Unitas' impressive understudy, generally considered the league's top backup. This move pushed Kilmer down to third man on the totem pole. But Kilmer fought it out, and when Wood injured his ankle in the third week of the pre-season during a win over Pittsburgh, the battle was down to two, Cuozzo and himself. Kilmer:

"The only doubt I ever had in my mind about playing was in New Orleans in 1967, and that had nothing to do with an injury. I had never played quarterback up until that time. I hadn't been established. If I hadn't done what I did in training camp and in my first few games, I'd probably have been cut. Call it fate, or stick-to-itiveness, or just doing my job, but I got a chance to play and just built it up from there."

By opening day against the Los Angeles Rams, Kilmer had built himself up to the starting quarterback position. Over the next four seasons he continued to build, accounting for 50 Saints touchdowns (47 passing, 3 rushing), while passing for nearly 7,500 yards and helping to firmly establish New Orleans as a big-time NFL city.

During that inaugural campaign Kilmer split time with Cuozzo. Statistically the two were very close, but stylistically they were worlds apart. As a Colt, Cuozzo had been so thoroughly schooled by Johnny U. that he actually resembled him, dropping back quickly, with efficient, well-timed steps, standing tall in the pocket, arm cocked and loaded, and firing off crisp spirals.

In stark contrast, Kilmer's style, more often than not, resembled that of a rugby player with a helmet. Rolling out of the pocket, scrambling for his life, or dropping back clutching the ball with both hands at waist level, squinting out over the defense as if staring into a stiff wind, while nervously shifting his weight back and forth from leg to leg, then heaving a pass from the hip. And those passes! They were described as everything from knuckleballs to dying quails. But while Kilmer was christened the "inventor of the wobbly pass," he was in actuality the perfecter of it.

During a 48-21 loss in Philadelphia in week 10 of that first season, Kilmer, who threw two touchdowns while relieving Cuozzo, teamed up with "Flea" Roberts for a Saints record 96-yard pass completion that carried from the Saints' three-yard line to the Eagles' one. The following week, with the Saints trailing 21-10 at the half, head coach Tom Fears inserted Kilmer into the lineup to replace Cuozzo. Kilmer promptly led the Saints 53 yards with the second half kickoff, capped off by Randy Schultz' 22-yard touchdown run. The Saints defense stiffened, and with just over four minutes left in the contest New Orleans got the ball back, still trailing 24-20. Starting at his own three-yard line, Kilmer marched the Saints 97 yards to the decisive touchdown. It was a seven-yard pass to tight end Kent Kramer with only 48 seconds remaining, delighting the 83,437 screaming fans who had packed Tulane Stadium.

In Washington three weeks later during the final game of the 1967 season, Kilmer once again was summoned from

While quarterbacking the Saints in their infancy, 1967-1970, Billy Kilmer threw for 7,490 yards and 47 touchdowns, leading them to the best expansion team record in NFL history.

the bench. This time the call came after a scoreless first quarter, and Kilmer connected with Danny Abramowicz on two touchdown tosses, one covering 80 yards, as the Saints won their third game of the season, 30-14 over the surprised Redskins.

Kilmer had led the Saints to two of their three victories, while assuming on-field command of the team and winning the hearts of the Tulane Stadium faithful. By season's end there was no room left for Cuozzo, and the Saints traded him to Minnesota for number one draft choices in '68 and '69, which New Orleans then used to draft Kevin Hardy and John Shinners.

In their sophomore season of 1968 Kilmer led the Saints to a 4-9-1 record, passing for more than 2,000 yards and throwing two touchdowns in six different games. Kilmer missed two full games during the '68 campaign due to a hairline fractured ankle. He was spelled by Karl Sweetan and Ronnie Lee South, but he returned to the lineup and saved his best performance for the home fans and the final game of the season. "Ol' Whiskey" passed for a team record 292 yards and two touchdowns as the Saints won their fourth game of 1968, 24-14 over the Pittsburgh Steelers.

As the Saints headed into the 1969 season the future looked promising. In two seasons they had compiled a 7-20-1 mark, the best ever for an expansion team, and had assembled some fine talent, including offensive standouts like wide receiver Danny Abramowicz, running backs Tony Baker and Andy Livingston, and lineman Del Williams and Jake Kupp. The defense was still anchored by veteran stalwarts like Doug Atkins and Dave "Weasel" Whitsell, along with some fresh faces like Dave Rowe and Mike Tilleman. The new kicker, Tom Dempsey, could regularly convert field goals from more than 50 yards. Even with all of that talent, the spark that fired the Saints engine was still Billy Kilmer, who was coming off of a 17-touchdown season (15 passing, 2 rushing). With plenty of offensive firepower at his disposal, everyone was anticipating big results.

But the Saints stumbled out of the gate in 1969, losing their first six games. Three of the losses were by six points or less, but Kilmer had only five touchdown passes to his credit. The Saints just couldn't seem to find the right place or the right time to put it all together.

They found both on Sunday, November 2, 1969 in St. Louis, a date which would fill the Saints' record book for years to come. Kilmer's adversary that day was Cardinal quarterback Charley Johnson, who had rejoined his teammates after a hitch in the Army, and had regained his starting position during training camp.

The Saints wasted no time declaring war on the Cards as Kilmer hit Dave Parks with a 25-yard touchdown pass in the first quarter to begin the scoring festival. Johnson answered with two scoring strikes to wide receiver Dave Williams, before Tom Dempsey kicked a 43-yard field goal to pull the Saints close at 14-10. Kilmer followed that with two more touchdown passes of his own, a 20-yarder to Ernie "The Wheel" Wheelwright and a five-yarder to Danny Abramowicz, to push the Saints ahead 23-14 at halftime. As the third quarter began, Kilmer continued the aerial onslaught, connecting with running back Don Shy for a 28-yard score before "The Wheel" rolled the Saints lead up to 37-14 with a one-yard run. But Charley Johnson wasn't nearly finished. He picked up the gauntlet that Kilmer had thrown at his feet and found ex-Saint John Gilliam with a 28-yard touchdown toss. Kilmer came right back, teaming up with Abramowicz again, this time from 11 yards out for a 44-21 Saints margin at the end of three quarters. Kilmer opened the fourth quarter by throwing his sixth touchdown pass of the day, finding Parks from the 13-yard line for his final tally of the historic contest. After Dempsey's conversion, the Saints led 51-21. Most opponents would have called it a day and began thinking of excuses to satisfy the media. But not Charley Johnson. The air was filled with footballs as he furiously led the Cardinals down the field three more times, throwing three more touchdowns, two of them to his favorite target of the day, Dave

Williams. Johnson finished the contest with six scoring passes also, but the Cardinals roaring comeback fell short of Kilmer and the Saints, as the electrifying aerial circus ended at 51-42.

"Kilmer and Johnson's Airshow" set an NFL record for most total touchdown passes in one game (12), along with five Saints' team records: most first downs (26), most total offensive yards (508), most passing yards (345), most points (51), and most PATs (6). Kilmer's 22 of 32, 345-yard, 6-touchdown performance was his best as a Saint and earned him NFL Player of the Week honors, while lighting a fire under the entire New Orleans team.

But the game that really symbolized Kilmer's four-year stand in New Orleans occurred three weeks later in Tulane Stadium versus his old team, the 49ers. Trailing by three touchdowns in the second quarter, Kilmer began leading the Saints back before the San Francisco defense exacted revenge on their former teammate's left arm, separating his shoulder.

Ed Khayat, Saints assistant coach, remembers the day:

"Billy came off all bent over to one side. We all figured he was done, but he said, 'Hell no! Pop it back into place and get me back out there.' They strapped him up and he was back out for the next series. We were losing 21-0 when he got hurt, but we won the game in spite of the bad shoulder. Frisco kept clobbering him on the side all day, but Bill just got right back up and threw another pass. He's one tough son of a gun."

The battered and bandaged Kilmer threw for 235 yards and two touchdowns as the Saints won another wild one 43-38, on their way to an eventual 5-9 finish, raising their three-year total to 12-29-1, which continued to be the NFL expansion team record.

The Saints won five of their final eight games in 1969 and Kilmer had his best Saints season, throwing for more than 2,500 yards and connecting for a Saints record 20 touchdowns.

But the promise of 1969 failed to materialize in 1970.

"We were building a good foundation. A fairly old, but good

defense, and a helluva offense in '69. Just before the 1970 season, Tom Fears and Vic Schwenk (general manager) started having fights over personnel. When that happened everything crumbled in one year," Kilmer recalls.

With the Saints off to a 1-5-1 start in 1970, John Mecom Jr. replaced head coach Tom Fears with J.D. Roberts, and the Saints limped in with a franchise worst 2-11-1 record. Kilmer started 10 games during the season, while fending off second-year backup Edd Hargett, and in January of 1971 he was traded to Washington for linebacker Tom Rousell and two draft choices, effectively clearing the decks for the arrival of the Archie Manning era.

In Washington where George Allen's "The Future is Now" slogan meant trading for battle-tested veterans and instantly molding them into a winner, Kilmer became a superstar, quarterbacking the Skins in the playoffs in his first season there. In his second season, "Ol' Whiskey" led Allen's "Over the Hill Gang" to the 1972 NFC title and a berth in Super Bowl VII. He steered Washington into post-season play three out of the next four seasons before retiring from professional football in 1978 after a 17-year career.

Billy Kilmer's determination and courage embodied the spirit of the early swashbuckling Saints, and carved out a special place for him in the hearts of New Orleans fans, who, in turn, carved out a special place in Kilmer's own heart for them.

"This city gave me a new lease on life and a chance to prove that I could play football. My whole career was reborn. It led me to Washington and playing in the Super Bowl for the Redskins. I always loved New Orleans, and I always will. I love the fans and the way they supported the team even when we lost. I used to tell the players, 'You don't realize how good you have it here. Put out, work a little harder, win a few games and you'll be kings of Louisiana.' I would have loved to have finished the job here, and brought a winner here. It would have been Mardi Gras for years."

Clutch receiver Danny Abramowicz catches a pass in a game against Dallas. Abramowicz was the Saints' seventeenth and final-round draft choice in 1967. When head coach Tom Fears tried to cut the rookie wide receiver, Abramowicz refused to leave. Fears gave him a second chance, and Abramowicz gave New Orleans a hero. In 1969 he led the entire NFL with 73 catches for 1,015 yards and seven touchdowns.

Every Boy's Hero

1967 - 1973

In the summer of 1967 New Orleans was giving birth not only to a football team named the Saints but also a football legend named Danny Abramowicz.

Abramowicz was drafted by the Saints out of Ohio's Xavier University, almost as an afterthought, in the 17th and final round. A wide receiver at 6 foot 1, 195 pounds, he was considered too small and slow to have a legitimate shot at the NFL. But all Danny wanted was a chance.

"When I went to training camp, Coach Fears was the head coach," Abramowicz recalls. "We trained in San Diego, and all I asked him for was an opportunity to make the team, a fair chance. He said he would, but after about three or four weeks of camp, I was mostly on special teams, and had gone through numerous roommates. We had a lot of guys coming through; it was like the last stop for the veteran type of guys, and all the cuts from other camps. So one day 'the turk' came to see me.

The knock comes on the door, and he says, 'Bring your playbook; coach wants to see you.' In other words, 'You're fired.' So I left my playbook, and I went downstairs and burst into his office and said, 'You never gave me a chance; you told me you were gonna give me a chance.' And he sort of was stunned, and he looked up at me and he said, 'You're serious.' I said 'I'm as serious as a heart attack,' and he said 'OK, I'll give you another chance.' So when I walked out, I sorta went 'Whew, that one worked.'"

Abramowicz started the next game against the 49ers in Portland, Oregon, and caught five passes in the first half. Three weeks later, when John Gilliam returned the regular season's opening kickoff 94 yards for a touchdown, not only was Danny on the Saint's roster, but he threw the block that sprung Gilliam's run into Saints folklore.

Abramowicz: "Gilliam's kickoff, at the time it happened, just going into a stadium with that many people, 85,000 people...I was used to playing in a stadium in college with 5,000, 6,000 people. Maybe for a big game we'd get 10 or 12,000. So just being out there was enough. But who would have ever dreamed that on the opening kickoff, of the opening game of a franchise, that a guy would run all the way for a touchdown, and you'd have a key block in the game. It was exciting, and it remained that way. The games just got more exciting, and the fans, I had never seen that type of support."

Abramowicz had caught only nine passes in the first six games of the Saints' inaugural season, but in week seven, in his first NFL start, he caught 12 against the Pittsburgh Steelers, and the position was his for the rest of his career.

Danny led the Saints in receiving from 1967 through 1971. In 1969 he led the entire NFL with 73 catches for more than 1,000 yards, as the Saints finished with their best record yet, 5-9.

In 1970 Abramowicz witnessed Tom Dempsey's record 63-yard field goal firsthand.

"Dempsey's kick was phenomenal if you really think about it, even up to this day. The guy kicked the ball 63 yards! I remember I was on the sidelines as they were lining up to kick the field goal, and I said, 'We've gotta be totally out of our minds.' In fact, I started walking down the sidelines, heading to the locker room. I never dreamed in my wildest imagination that he could make that kick. Once I saw the ball, it sort of took a funny flutter, and then it took off, and when it made it through the uprights, of course, I ran back up the field and acted like I knew all along that we were gonna make the field goal. What a game of excitement. The stadium went crazy, the players went crazy, the guy on the radio doing the broadcast, Al Wester, lost power. The game was ironic because we really kicked their butts the whole game and they came back at the end and scored and took the lead, and to come back and put a finish on like that was tremendous. It's one of the moments you'll never forget as you look back over your football career. Phenomenal."

Abramowicz led all Saints in scoring in 1972 with seven touchdowns, but in 1973 was traded to the San Francisco 49ers, where he continued his NFL record streak of catching at least one pass in 105 consecutive games. Danny retired from the 49ers after the '74 season, but his heart had never really left New Orleans.

"I just never did feel comfortable in a San Francisco uniform. If I had it to do over again, I'd have stayed here. I'd have played out my career here. It just shows you how a community can grow on you, how you can get a love for a city. I fell in love with the city, and I think the city fell in love with me," Abramowicz says.

Danny Abramowicz was every boy's hero, a classic long shot who hit the bull's-eye. The Saints' last-round draft choice in 1967, considered too small and too slow to end up in the NFL, ended up All Pro and leading the league in receptions.

Abramowicz played for the Saints from 1967 through two games of the 1973 season. He caught 309 passes, had 10 games with more than 100 yards receiving, and his 37 touchdowns and 4,875 yards receiving were club records.

In July of 1988, to no one's surprise, Abramowicz, along

with Archie Manning, was one of the first two players inducted into the brand new Saints Hall of Fame in Kenner, Louisiana. It was a fitting tribute to Danny's efforts, as he put it, a permanent "thank you" for giving all that he had.

Through the years, Abramowicz maintained his home in New Orleans, raised his family here, and became head football coach at Jesuit High School, giving back something to the youth of a city that gave so much to him on countless, record-setting, sun-drenched Sundays in Tulane Stadium.

Abramowicz: "When I think back to the early years of the Saints, there was a magic to it. You'd look at the old Tulane Stadium when we'd go out to a game. Many times we'd leave early for the stadium, and we'd go out there and there would already be 10, 15,000 people in the stadium. I mean, everywhere else we went, there would be nowhere near that amount. There was a charisma, there was something in the stands here. The fans were excited, and they were exciting. They looked forward to that Sunday to go to Tulane Stadium, with all the traffic jams, and no place to park, hot, rain. It didn't make any difference. They were just into it. And I think that the players were into it also. I think they really enjoyed playing. Yes, it was a job. It was a big business, but we sort of set that aside, and we just enjoyed playing. The fans made it fun. When we lost, you felt just as bad for the fans as you did for yourself that you let them down. I don't know if it was the mystique of Tulane Stadium, or the newness of the franchise, or exactly what made that magic. I don't know what it was; I can't put my finger on it. But I'll never forget it as long as I live."

And the people of Louisiana will never forget Danny Abramowicz, the original Saint.

Old Warriors, New Battlefield

1967 - 1968

                Retiring a player's jersey is one of the highest compliments a team can pay. Due to practicality, it isn't done often. In the case of the Saints, it has only happened twice. You won't find numbers 31 or 81 on the Saints roster ever again, out of respect for the players who originally wore them, running back Jim Taylor, number 31, and defensive end Doug Atkins, number 81.

    Both players were members of the original Saints in 1967, finished out their careers in New Orleans, and were later voted into the Pro Football Hall of Fame.

    Taylor played only two seasons at Louisiana State University, but he became an All-American and the first player in Southeast Conference history to lead the conference in scoring for two successive years. He was the second-round pick of the Green Bay Packers in 1958. In 1959 coach Vince Lombardi

Rare photos of Jim Taylor (31) and Doug Atkins (81) hang in the Saints Hall of Fame Museum in Kenner, honoring the only two Saints players to ever have their jersey numbers retired. Taylor led the Saints in rushing during their inaugural season, while Atkins helped establish the character of the tough Saints defense.

arrived, and the rest is history. Taylor set an NFL rushing record with five consecutive 1,000-yard seasons, from 1960 through 1964, and helped the Packers to four NFL titles before playing out his option and signing with the expansion Saints in 1967.

Like a returning gladiator, Taylor was the last player introduced in Tulane Stadium before the Saints inaugural home opener against Los Angeles, and the roar of the crowd was deafening. He justified the hero's welcome by leading the Saints in rushing, with 390 yards, and finishing second in receiving with 38 catches. Taylor also scored two touchdowns while fighting nagging injuries, which would force his retirement only five days before the 1968 regular season opener.

Doug Atkins was a 6-foot 8-inch, 270-pound defensive end who arrived at Tennessee as a basketball player and left in 1953 as an All-American football player and the number one

Doug "The Mountain" Atkins (81) brought to the young Saints a brutal style of defense. Following a game in 1967, he remarked to Cowboy quarterback Craig Morton, "Well, we lost the game, but you'll be sore tomorrow." Morton didn't disagree with him.

draft choice of the NFL's Cleveland Browns. In 1955 he was traded to the Chicago Bears, where he became a living legend as one of the NFL's all-time great defenders. By 1967 he was unhappy in Chicago and, after requesting to be traded, "The Mountain," as he was called, moved south to New Orleans, where his feats of superhuman strength continued. Such as the time when he reportedly lifted up a Dallas offensive lineman and literally threw him onto startled Cowboy quarterback Don Meredith. It was a play that typified the rough and wreckless attitude that Atkins instilled into the young Saints defenders during his three seasons as their on-the-field leader, before his retirement in 1969.

Number 31, Jim Taylor, and number 81, Doug Atkins, are two warriors from a bygone era of Saints football, gone but not forgotten. Just check the rosters.

When Hats Were Black

1969 Pre-season

In 1969 Saints owner John Mecom Jr. wanted a new look for his team's third NFL season. Since their inception, the Saints had worn beautiful gold numerals on white or black jerseys, gold pants, and gold helmets with a black *fleur de lis* symbol on each side.

But they were about to make the most controversial and short-lived uniform change in their history. For the 1969 pre-season, Mecom sent his troops out wearing black helmets with a gold *fleur de lis* on each side. It was a mistake. To begin with, Mecom had failed to register the black helmets with the NFL office. The league's entire line of merchandise represented the Saints with gold helmets, so the league wouldn't license the black helmets.

Faced with pressure from the league office, and poor fan response, Mecom quickly decided to scrub the idea. He found himself with a locker room full of black Saints helmets. At the time, the NFL was still operating a type of farm system as

Head coach Tom Fears instructs guard John Shinners during the 1969 pre-season, the time when the Saints experimented with black helmets. However, due to the fact that the NFL's entire merchandising line represented the Saints with gold helmets, the black hat lasted only as long as it took to get more gold ones shipped in.

feeders for NFL clubs. The Saints' farm team was the Richmond Roadrunners, coached by J.D. Roberts, who in 1970 would replace Tom Fears, becoming the Saints' second head coach. Mecom shipped the entire batch of black helmets to Richmond, and the Saints were back in their familiar gold helmets for the 1969 season opener against Washington.

But the black hat fiasco wasn't the only uniform trouble the early Saints had. The thickness of the gold numerals on the jerseys varied from player to player, and sometimes from week to week. It seems that when torn jerseys were reordered, some arrived with wide numerals and some with narrow ones -- which, by the end of the long, tough season, left the Saints resembling high-class barnstormers. This problem, along with the difficulty broadcasters had reading the shiny gold numbers off of the white jerseys on sunny afternoons, led to the Saints discontinuing use of the gold numerals after the 1969 season.

The old gold pants remained in use until 1975, when the Saints celebrated the opening of their new Superdome home by changing to white pants, which when worn with their white jerseys created an unspectacular and unpopular look.

The following year, 1976, Hank Stram came to town to coach the team, and the Saints, in the tradition of Stram's great Kansas City teams, began wearing black pants with their white jerseys. This continued until 1986, when new owner Tom Benson brought back a shiny version of the old gold pants for Jim Mora's first season as head coach.

So the Saints' gold helmet remains the one constant through a quarter of a century of regular season battles. Seasoned New Orleans football fans still smile fondly when recalling the summer of 1969, when the Saints put a new twist on an old adage, as the good guys wore the black hats.

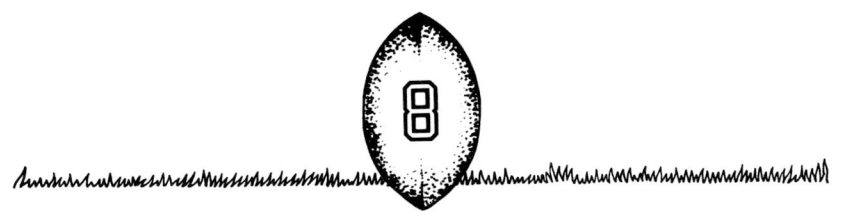

'Thunderfoot'

Tom Dempsey 1969 - 1970

Place-kicker Tom Dempsey came to the Saints in 1969 as a free agent. Though he spent only two of his eventful 11 NFL seasons in New Orleans, in the memories of NFL fans he is forever linked to the Saints--and one unforgettable, record-shattering Sunday afternoon in Tulane Stadium.

Despite being born with half a right foot and only two fingers on his right hand, Dempsey excelled in sports. In high school he played defensive end. At California's Palomar Junior College he was a shot-putter and wrestler, along with playing both offense and defense on the football field. It was at Palomar that Dempsey first took up place-kicking, and after a stint in the Atlantic Coast Football League, his kicking got him a ride on the San Diego Chargers taxi squad in 1968.

In 1969 coach Tom Fears brought Dempsey to the Saints, where he made All Pro while setting a team scoring record of 99 points, which stood for 16 years. Known as "Thunderfoot," Dempsey thrilled the fans with four field goals in each of the wins over the Eagles and Giants, and with a 55-yarder against the Rams, just shy of the 56-yard NFL record.

But the best was yet to come.

Halfway through the 1970 season, having won only once, the Saints replaced head coach Tom Fears with J.D. Roberts and prepared to face the playoff-bound Detroit Lions. Three Dempsey field goals and two interceptions by linebacker Jackie Burkett kept the Saints ahead, 16-14, but when Detroit's Errol Mann hit a field goal with 18 seconds left, it seemed the Saints' luck had run out.

Tom Dempsey recalls the situation, and what happened next.

"It was a very strange game. No one knew how we were gonna play (because of the coaching change), but the team actually played very well. We probably played our best game of the year. We fought them nip and tuck the whole game and then they went ahead on a field goal. They kicked off to Al Dodd and Al ran it back. Then Al caught a pass from Billy Kilmer, about a 10- or 15-yard out, right on the sidelines. It was a great throw and catch to set up the 63-yard field goal.

"I knew that I could kick the ball that far. It was very humid that particular day, we didn't have a whole lot of wind, and on humid days the ball didn't really carry that well in Tulane Stadium. But I knew when I hit it, that I hit it good enough to carry. Whether or not it'd stay straight -- that was the question. We got a perfect snap from Jackie Burkett, and Joe Scarpati made a perfect hold and we had great protection from the line. What happens with field goals is, it's like hitting a golf ball, and I hit that one as sweet as you could hit it."

Dempsey's NFL record 63-yard field goal with two seconds left, cleared the crossbar with about 18 inches to spare. As the old Sugar Bowl rocked in the delirium of an unbelievable 19-17 Saints victory, Tom Dempsey rode the shoulders of his teammates from the overcast brown dirt field, and into football immortality.

Four weeks later in Los Angeles, Dempsey booted two field goals from more than 50 yards, but the Saints failed to win

Tom Dempsey, born with half a right foot and a withered right hand, kicks the longest field goal in NFL history, 63 yards, on November 8, 1970, to beat the Detroit Lions, 19-17. Jackie Burkett, who snapped the ball that day, remembers the kick: "It sounded like some kind of explosion. It was almost like the ball grunted."

another game all season. Their franchise low 2-11-1 record secured them the right to draft Archie Manning.

Dempsey left the Saints following that 1970 season, making stops in Philadelphia, where he hit six field goals in one game, Los Angeles, where his kicking helped propel the Rams into two NFC title games, Houston, and Buffalo. Before retiring in 1979, Dempsey, who reportedly kicked 70-yarders in practice, hit 12 field goals of 50 yards or better.

But none could ever top the 63-yard rainbow of November 8, 1970.

Archie Is A Saint

1971

Never in the history of the Saints has a player arrived amid such fanfare, or facing such superhuman expectations, as quarterback Archie Manning in 1971.

During his fabled All-American career at Ole Miss, Manning had been elevated to Southern folk-hero status, with his Rebel exploits romanticized in the popular song "The Ballad of Archie Who" and his boyish face adorning tens of thousands of "Archie Who" buttons. Only a fractured forearm in his senior season seemed to deny Archie's Heisman Trophy hopes. His Ole Miss coach, Johnny Vaught, predicted that Archie, with his cannon arm and sprint out style, would "revolutionize professional football."

This was the legend that preceded SuperManning's arrival in New Orleans. Archie remembers it well:

"I think when I first came there was a lot of pressure on me, although I'm not sure that I realized it at the time. It was kind of in a blaze of glory, I guess, from all of the things that had

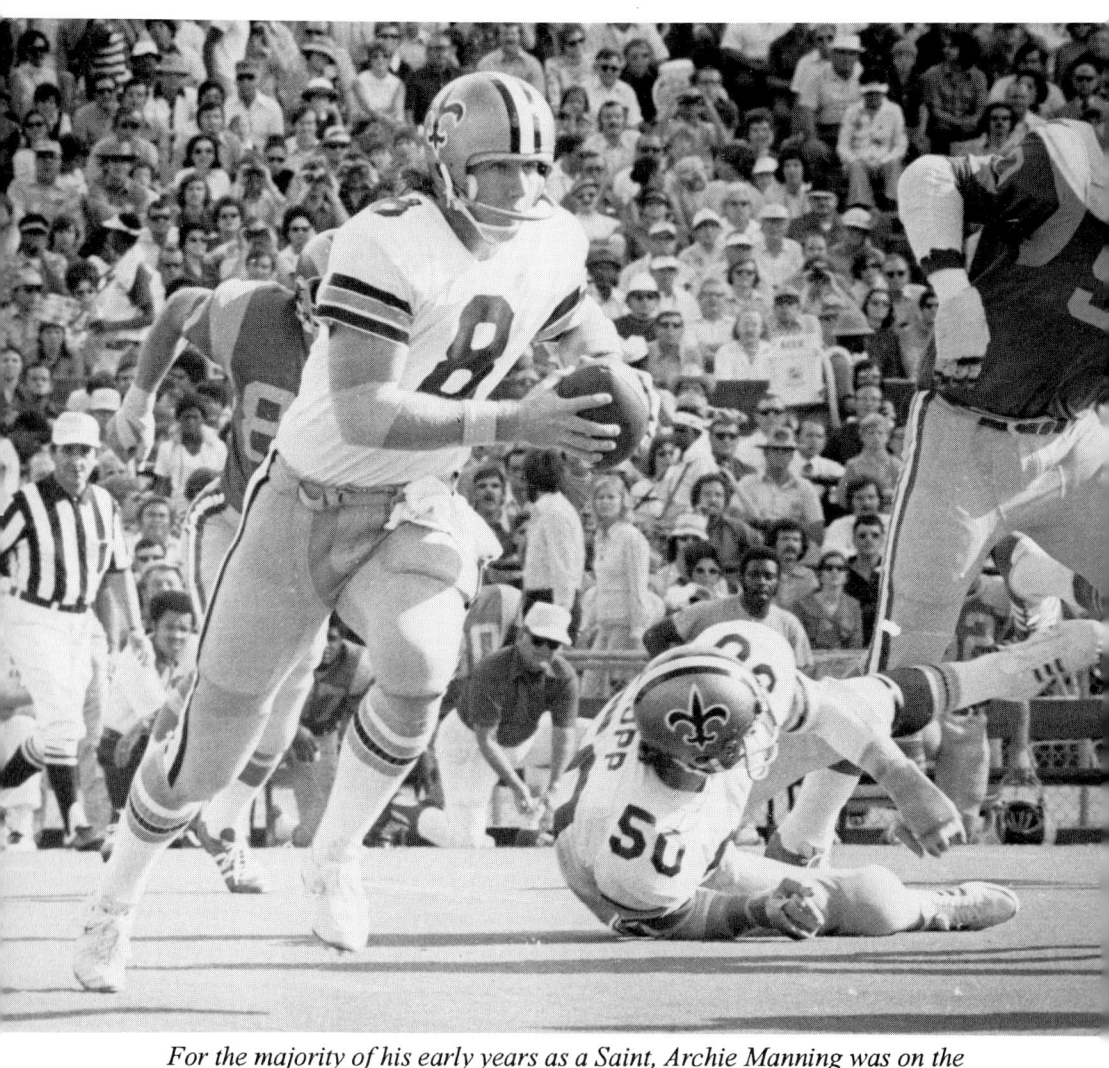

For the majority of his early years as a Saint, Archie Manning was on the run, as in this game with the Los Angeles Rams. In an earlier game against the Rams, during his first NFL start, he led the Saints to a victory, running in the winning TD as time ran out.

happened at Ole Miss, all the notoriety there. And I guess it was magnified here somewhat, in that we'd played big games against LSU. It was a great rivalry. Then I'd also played in the Sugar Bowl against Arkansas in 1970.

"I think the Saints fans and the media felt like the Saints needed a quarterback, and that was 'the year of the quarterback,' when Jim Plunkett, myself and Dan Pastorini were the first three picks. So, New Orleans is where I wanted to come, and fortunately I was selected by them. So it was a real exciting time, although, as I said before, I think I was still wrapped up in all this hoopla from my days at Ole Miss."

The Saints finished 4-8-2 in Manning's rookie season, including a 24-14 upset over eventual Super Bowl champion Dallas, when Archie ran for two scores. But nothing came close to Manning's NFL debut. He passed for a score, and as the final horn sounded, he ran in the winning touchdown from one yard out in a 24-20 opening day victory over the Rams.

"Well, believe me, my eyes were big, playing in my first NFL football game. To be able to start in my first game as a professional, and then we were playing the Rams, who were kingpins of our division. And then add to that, that during our pre-season we lost all six games. We were 0 and 6, and the Rams, of course, were heavy favorites. The big crowd in Tulane Stadium. I think it was the hottest game I've ever played in, and I think the heat affected the Rams somewhat. Of course, it affected us, too, I think. But to be able to beat them, in somewhat of a dramatic fashion, on the last play of the game..."

In 1972, his second season with the Saints, quarterback Archie Manning took the snap on every offensive play, throwing and completing more passes than any other NFL signal-caller, and subsequently wiping out most Saints single-season passing marks. But following his 18 touchdown passes in 1972, Archie suffered a string of nagging injuries, which, when not sidelining him, frequently kept him from operating at full strength over the next five seasons. Archie remembers the frustration:

"Looking back on it, I think everybody has injuries, and I

think you have to be fortunate if you can still play. Adrenaline is a great thing. If you're healthy enough to be able to kind of answer the bell and begin a game, it's amazing what adrenaline will do to carry you through the game. Football is a very physical game, it's very tough, and everybody's hurt. So, overall, I didn't really have to miss that many games. I had some injuries, and I think that sometimes the injuries to quarterbacks are blown out of proportion. Although the times that you do have to miss are very, very frustrating. I thought football, and pro football, was a lot of fun. But to be hurt was the real frustrating part of it. Losing is tough, but being hurt and not being able to participate really works on your mind and makes for some extremely long weeks."

Besides the injuries, in 1974 something new threatened to permanently remove Archie from the Saints lineup: A bona fide million dollar offer from the Memphis Southmen of the new World Football League. He explains:

"Some things were happening in Memphis, which was very close to home, very close to Ole Miss. And not that I got tired of New Orleans. I mean everybody gets tired of losing, but I'd never had any problems with anything going on in New Orleans. Overall, considering the way we played, and the type of teams we had, the people here, the media, people here treated me very good. But this team was in Memphis and we'd made contact with the owner up there, John Basset, and they'd put out these big contracts to Larry Csonka and Jim Kiick, and I was actually represented by the same people in those days. And so they just talked to us about something that was very attractive, and also I'd be playing in Memphis.

"But what was not attractive about it was that I had two years to run on my Saints contract, and I did not want to be a lame duck quarterback in New Orleans. I knew our days were tough, and Sundays could be long, and I just didn't want to be out of favor with the fans....I knew that it would be virtually impossible to play. So, that's the reason that I really didn't do it."

Black Sunday

September 16, 1973

When head coach John North took over from J. D. Roberts with only two games remaining in the 1973 pre-season, he knew it would be a scramble to get his staff and players ready for the season opener. But after a 16-10 win over Houston in the final pre-season tune-up, it seemed like North just might pull it off.

Besides being North's NFL head coaching debut, opening day 1973 had an added attraction for Saints fans -- the opponent would be arch-rival Atlanta. The Saints/Falcons feud had developed naturally and with good reason. The geographic proximity of the two cities, coupled with the fact that the Falcons had entered the league only one season prior to the Saints' entry, created ideal conditions for the spawning of a genuine rivalry.

These seeds began to sprout in 1967's final pre-season contest, when the infant Saints defeated the Falcons, 27-14, in their first ever appearance before their hometown fans. But the rivalry burst into full bloom on the green grass of Tulane Stadium during the first official meeting between the two teams, in week 11 of the Saints' inaugural season. In a game advertised as the "Battle for Southern Football Supremacy," Atlanta jumped out to a 21-3 lead before Saints quarterback Billy Kilmer came off of the bench to replace Gary Cuozzo and lead New Orleans back. Trailing 24-20 with just over four minutes left, Kilmer marched the Saints 97 yards to victory, the winning score coming on a seven-yard pass that tight end Kent Kramer one-handed in the Falcon end zone with just 48 seconds remaining in the contest.

Following those initial Saints triumphs, the Falcons took a 45-17 victory in 1969. The NFL's realignment in 1970 placed both teams together in the NFC's Western Division, where, like feuding cousins, the Deep South rivals would do battle in a yearly home and away series, which Atlanta proceeded to sweep each season leading up to the 1973 opener.

Sunday, September 16, 1973, "Black Sunday" to the Saints faithful, began calmly enough with a scoreless first quarter. But early in the second, the Falcons scored the first of their eventual eight touchdowns, and cruised to a 24-0 halftime lead. It was 31-0 before Saints quarterback Archie Manning hit running back Bill Butler with a five-yard pass for New Orleans' only score. But the Falcons were only half finished with their pinball scoring. Helped by six interceptions, they continued to pour it on the hapless Saints. But to New Orleans fans, the final straw was when the soaring Falcons turned defeat into humiliation by firing off four passes on their final five plays, connecting on one for yet another touchdown.

The 62-7 embarrassment was by far the darkest hour in Saints history. In the minds of New Orleans fans, it would be years before the memory could be displaced -- five years to be exact.

Squeezing 'The Juice'

November 4, 1973

After the most disastrous start in the history of the franchise -- a 62-7 opening day blowout by the Atlanta Falcons and a 40-3, nationally televised, Monday night dumping by the Dallas Cowboys -- Saints fans braced themselves for what promised to be the longest and most painful campaign yet, the 1973 season.

But as quickly as the season seemingly spiraled out of control, first-year head coach John North managed to settle his troops and split their next four games, to stand at 2-4 with eight weeks remaining. Even so, no one could have expected what transpired over the next two weeks. The club that had displayed virtually no defense while yielding 102 points in their first two outings, allowed a grand total of one field goal against two of the NFL's premiere offenses.

First up were the defending NFC champion Washington

Redskins, on the way to their third straight playoff appearance. The Saints held the NFL's most valuable player, Larry Brown, to six yards rushing -- and the entire Redskin team to just 18 more. Washington quarterbacks Bill Kilmer and Sonny Jurgensen were sacked five times and gave up a pair of interceptions as New Orleans won, 19-3.

The next opponent to run up against the Saints' newly constructed brick wall was the Buffalo Bills and O.J. Simpson. Simpson was on his way to an eventual NFL record 2,003 yards rushing and was expected to continue his record pace in New Orleans. The largest Saints crowd of the year, nearly 75,000, watched in amazement as the Saints' defense stuffed O.J., holding him to 79 yards on 20 carries -- and registering the first shutout in New Orleans history, 13-0. It was one of only two times all year that "the Juice" failed to break the 100-yard mark.

The whole afternoon was summed up on his final carry. Desperately needing a touchdown, the Bills faced a fourth and one from the Saints 11. Everyone knew O.J. was coming, but Saints Jim Merlo, Jerry Moore and Ernie Jackson swarmed over the Buffalo workhorse for no gain, and the Bills never threatened again.

For the first time in franchise history, the Saints stood even at the midway point of a season. And even though they'd eventually finish at 5-9, fans would long remember two Sundays in September when the roaring chant of "defense" filled Tulane Stadium as the Saints stopped the Redskins and squeezed "the Juice."

Saints head coach John North exhorts his defense to hold one more time. In 1973, after allowing 102 points in the first two games of the season, the Saints defense came to life and recorded the first shutout in team history, 13-0 over Buffalo, holding O.J. Simpson to only 79 yards during his NFL record-setting 2,003-yard season.

A Victory For The Fans

October 27, 1974

The Saints were a troubled team with troubled fans in 1974. Coming off of a club record-tying 5-9 mark in 1973, fans couldn't wait to begin cheering for head coach John North's second NFL campaign. But they'd have to.

First, a players' strike forced the NFL to play their initial two pre-season games without the veterans. Then, the future of Saints quarterback Archie Manning was clouded by a bona fide million dollar offer from the Memphis Southmen of the new World Football League.

The fans were still waiting for something to cheer about, as the Saints stumbled out of the gate headfirst into controversy. After a 1-4 start, owner John Mecom Jr. reportedly told North to bench Manning. The following week, backup quarterbacks Bobby Scott and rookie Larry Cipa led the Saints to a 13-3 victory over Atlanta. After the win, it came to light that Manning was reportedly on the trading block and on his way to the Falcons. The Saints were now knee-deep in an uncer-

A 22-minute booing, the longest in NFL history, was conducted by Saints fans in Tulane Stadium during a 14-10 victory over Philadelphia in 1974. With no end in sight to the thunderous cascade of noise, the Eagles flubbed a play and were forced to settle for a field goal, and an eventual loss.

tainty that further bewildered their fans, some of whom felt Manning was being discarded merely for entertaining the offer from the World Football League.

But before Manning could be dealt away, the Saints learned that a seemingly minor knee injury that Bobby Scott had suffered in the Falcons win would sideline him for the upcoming game with Philadelphia. So Manning was once again the starter.

The Saints fans who filled Tulane Stadium for the Eagles game were ready to explode with frustration. It was a helpless sense of frustration that was summed up by a sign which hung from the upper deck railing that read "Trade Mecom--not Manning."

The game was a struggle, but Manning tied it up at seven in the third quarter when he scored on a lateral from running back Jess Phillips on a broken play from the one.

Later in the quarter, the officials made a questionable personal foul call on Saints defensive tackle Elex Price, and the crowd got edgy. A few plays later, Saints linebacker Wayne Colman was flagged for the same infraction inside the Saints 10 yard line. The crowd snapped.

A huge tidal wave of boos rained down from the decks of the old stadium. The deafening roar continued non-stop and delayed the game for 22 minutes, forcing Eagles quarterback Roman Gabriel to finally waste a play, then settle for a field goal.

With less than three minutes remaining in the game, Manning took the Saints on their second 77-yard touchdown drive to win the game, 14-10. The headlines read, "Manning again proves himself number one."

Manning had indeed regained his familiar starting position, and the Saints had win number three of an eventual five that season, with a big assist from their fans and an NFL record 22-minute boo, which, according to Eagles head coach Mike McCormack, was the real story of the day.

"There's no question that it cost us the game," McCormack concluded.

The Hank Stram Era

1976 - 1977

Since their inception in 1967, the Saints had won only 32 games in 9 seasons. But in January of 1976, Saints owner John Mecom Jr. made what many observers felt was his first serious move toward NFL respectability.

He signed Hank Stram to a five-year head coaching contract. Stram's record was impressive. In 15 seasons with the Dallas Texans/Kansas City Chiefs franchise, he had won 124 games, three AFL titles and a Super Bowl, before leaving after the 1974 season.

The Saints were ready for a winner, and Stram was ready for a new challenge. It seemed the perfect match.

Stram: "I felt very enthusiastic about it. I thought that it was a great opportunity football-wise, plus we were very much involved with wanting to come to New Orleans. It was one of our favorite cities. I had a lot of great friends here, and I thought it was a tremendous challenge. I also thought that we had a great nucleus to begin with at the quarterback position, in the

Hank Stram became head coach of the Saints in 1976 and immediately began making over the team's image, including new uniforms. However, following two seasons at the helm, Stram was fired, having compiled a 7-21 record, which included 10 losses by a touchdown or less.

person of Archie Manning. At that time I had four different head coaching opportunities, one of which was at a major college, and the other three were in professional football. But because of the fact that we loved New Orleans so much, and were so enamored with the idea that we would have Archie Manning, I thought that this would be the place to come."

Stram went right to work. He drafted running backs Chuck Muncie and Tony Galbreath, numbers one and two, and dubbed the explosive tandem "Thunder and Lightning." Along with Manning and tight end Henry Childs, Stram considered the rookies two more stones in a foundation from which he would construct a new NFL powerhouse. But before Stram could begin building, a crack developed in the foundation's cornerstone.

"As I've said so many times, Archie Manning was a franchise player without a franchise during his career. As a result, he made things happen," Stram explains.

"I always felt very strongly that you couldn't win big unless you had a quarterback who could do it all, who had great escapability skill, and also could move by design, along with being able to throw from the pocket. Archie had all of those ingredients, was a tremendous leader, a big-play guy, and a big-play maker. So, the tough thing about it really was the fact that we didn't have Archie for...(a single) game in 1976. We certainly thought that he would be able to play, but it turned out that he had a problem with his right shoulder and we had to keep him out for the entire year. So that put a big hardship on our football team, and as a result our program was derailed by a year."

Stram's five-year plan to propel the Saints into the NFL's upper echelon depended on substantial contributions from Manning. But with an injured Archie watching the entire '76 season from the sidelines, Stram went to his backups.

Quarterbacks Bobby Scott and ex-Bear Bobby Douglas each passed for more than 1,000 yards, but the big offensive guns in Stram's first season in New Orleans were running backs Tony Galbreath and Chuck Muncie. His "Thunder and Lightning" combo did it all in their rookie season. Muncie, the lightning half, led the team in rushing and scored twice. Galbreath, the thunder half, led the Saints in receiving and rushed for seven touchdowns.

In week three, "Thunder and Lightning" struck simultaneously in Kansas City. Muncie rushed for 126 yards, Galbreath for 146 and two touchdowns, one a Saints record 74-yarder, as New Orleans claimed their first victory of the Hank Stram era, 27-17, over Stram's former team, the Chiefs. Stram recalls:

"It was the highlight of the year for all of us, very frankly. I think it's always kind of exciting to have an opportunity to go back and play against the team that you left, and as a result there was a lot of excitement about the game. We felt very good about the fact that we could go back there and beat them, especially beat them in Kansas City."

Two weeks later, Stram's troops stomped arch-rival Atlanta, 30-0, for the largest Saints victory margin ever. They later added a one-point win over the Lions, before tying a team scoring record with a 51-27 barnburner over the expansion

Seattle Seahawks. Stram's first Saints team broke 24 team records and finished at 4-10, with four of their 10 losses by a touchdown or less. It was improvement, but Stram wanted more.

"Well, very frankly, I had higher hopes and expectations for that first season. We knew that we were going to have to struggle, because of the loss of Archie Manning. But we felt that if we played like we were capable of playing, and didn't give games away, we'd have a chance to win more games than we actually did," Stram explains.

"It turned out that in the two years that we were here, we lost seven games by missed field goals and the kicking game. That really hurt us more than anything else that happened to our football team. It was just brutal the way we lost some games because of the kicking game."

The second year of the Hank Stram era promised continued steady improvement for the Saints, and a healthy Archie Manning seemed ready to lead the way.

Manning ran for three touchdowns and passed for another, as the Saints dumped the Bears, 42-24, on the third Sunday of the season. Manning was named NFL Player of the Week, but two weeks later was once again out of the lineup, this time due to an ankle injury.

As he did the previous season, Stram forged on by inserting quarterbacks Bobby Scott and Bobby Douglas. The Saints got their second win, a 27-26 upset over the Rams, on a fake field goal touchdown pass from holder Tom Blanchard to Elois Grooms.

Following a 10-7 overtime loss to the 49ers, Manning came off of the bench, and out of his four-week injury exile. He threw two second half touchdowns to Henry Childs, one with just over a minute left in the game, to defeat the rival Falcons, 21-20.

The next two weeks brought three-point losses to the 49ers and Jets before one of the most infamous Saints defeats. The

0-26 Tampa Bay Buccaneers used six interceptions, three of which they returned for touchdowns, to take their first NFL victory, 33-14, over the embarrassed Saints in the Superdome.

The Saints finished 1977 at 3-11, and six of their losses were, once again, by a touchdown or less. But if the won-loss record wasn't spectacular, the offensive arsenal that Stram had assembled certainly was.

Despite starting only nine games, Manning tied for fourth among NFC passers, throwing for eight scores and running for five more. Tight end Henry Childs set a team record with nine touchdown catches, and "Thunder and Lightning" continued to strike from the Saints backfield. Chuck Muncie scored seven touchdowns and set a new Saints rushing record with 811 yards, while Tony Galbreath rushed for 644 yards and led the team in catches with 41.

In two seasons Hank Stram had built the Saints into an explosive and competitive team, but before he could begin year three of his five-year plan, he was replaced by Dick Nolan as head coach of the Saints, after posting a 7-21 record in New Orleans. Stram comments:

"In the '77 season I thought we were making some progress, because we had Archie Manning healthy, and because Galbreath and Muncie had played another year together. We had some cohesion and consistency from an offensive standpoint. Also, we had been able to accumulate some defensive players that were starting to come on and help us.

"We just felt that the third year was going to be the crucial year, the pivotal year as to how much success we'd enjoy. We felt that we were on the right track, and we felt that we were making progress. I told Mr. Mecom when I took the job that we certainly wanted to win, but the ultimate goal was to win a Super Bowl. It was just unfortunate that it terminated after two years and we never had a chance to fulfill that dream."

Archie On Ice

1976-1977

When Hank Stram became head coach of the Saints in '76, for the first time in his NFL career, Archie Manning had a head coach with an offensive philosophy tailor-made for the explosive sprintout style that had propelled him to national prominence at Ole Miss.

According to Archie, his spirit was willing, but his arm was weak. He explains:

"I was very excited when Hank Stram was hired to come in and take over the football program. I'd had a good friendship with Hank, gotten to know Hank when I'd first come into the league. He was always really fond of me, and he and my college coach, Johnny Vaught, were real close. And from what Coach Vaught had told me, Hank had really tried to make some efforts to see if he could get me into the Kansas City program when I was coming out of Ole Miss. But they were drafting really far down in those days because they had won the Super Bowl right in 1970, just the year before.

"Hank used to love to talk football to me. He was a real

A dejected Archie Manning, taking a break on the bench, reflects the frustration shared by the team and fans during the early seventies. For much of his career, nagging injuries kept Archie either on the bench or operating below full capacity. During the Hank Stram era, 1976-1977, Archie started only 9 of 28 games.

innovator, and I think he was crazy about my ability to sprint out and move. I never will forget the night I kept hearing the rumors that he was going to be hired, and I'd heard that he was going to be hired the next day. This was right after the 1975 season.

"I found out how to get in touch with Hank that night, so I called him and I told him, 'Coach, I'm really excited about you coming, but I've got to tell you, my arm's no good. I've been messing with this thing for months now, and I can't even brush my teeth, because my arm hurts so bad.' Well, he had me on a plane the next morning, and for the next two weeks just seeing different doctors, and trying to decide what to do about this thing."

All Archie could do was undergo two tendonitis operations, then watch from the sidelines the entire season, as the first edition of Stram's Saints went 4-10.

Archie began the 1977 season healthy and productive, being named NFL Player of the Week as he ran for three touchdowns and passed for another in a 42-24 win in Chicago in week three.

Later an ankle injury sidelined Archie for four games before he came off the bench to throw two touchdowns in a 21-20 upset win over rival Atlanta.

Archie finished 1977 tied for fourth among NFC passers, but the Saints finished 3-11. And thanks to an impatient John Mecom Jr., Hank Stram's stay in New Orleans was over. Manning was unhappy about Stram's dismissal:

"I don't have a lot of regrets from football....But I do regret that I didn't really get a full chance with Hank Stram. I just felt like he had a great offensive mind, and I would have liked to have played more football for him."

'Thunder And Lightning'

1976 - 1980

In 1976, before his first draft as head coach of the New Orleans Saints, Hank Stram said he was looking for thunder and lightning. He found it in his first two draft picks, running backs Tony Galbreath and Chuck Muncie.

Stram recalls draft day 1976:

"It was a situation where we had several options as far as running backs were concerned that particular year. But in the final analysis, after careful survey and scouting and all the information that we got, we just felt that Chuck had so much natural ability. He was 6' 3" and weighed 235 and ran the 40 in 4.5.... The way it turned out,...in the second round Tony Galbreath was available, and we were fortunate enough to get him, too. So I gave them the name, 'Thunder and Lightning'."

Muncie, the Heisman trophy runner-up at California, and

Galbreath, the MVP at Missouri, were both the rare combination of a big back who could run with punishing power inside and graceful speed outside. In addition to their running skills, both had outstanding pass-catching abilities.

In their rookie season with the Saints, "Thunder and Lightning" entered the league with a bang, beginning a friendly competition that would fill the record books and thrill the fans.

Muncie, the lightning, led the team in rushing with 652 yards and two touchdowns. He also caught 31 passes and led all NFL rookies in yards gained.

Galbreath, the thunder, was the Saints' MVP, rushing for 570 yards, while scoring a team record-tying eight touchdowns. He also led the team in both receiving, with 54 catches, and kickoff returns.

Early in the 1976 season, "Thunder and Lightning" teamed up to bring Stram his first win as head coach of the Saints. In a 27-17 win over Stram's former team, the Kansas City Chiefs, Muncie rolled for 126 yards, while Galbreath piled up 146 yards and two touchdowns. As the season wore on, "Thunder and Lightning" were striking frequently, with both scoring touchdowns in the Saints 51-27 win over Seattle and in a 33-14 loss to the Rams in Los Angeles.

In its first season of implementation, Hank Stram's "Thunder and Lightning" attack produced impressive results and seemed right on course as the Saints finished 4-10 and prepared for campaign number two.

In 1977 they picked up right where they left off.

Galbreath started all 14 games at fullback, rushed for 644 yards, scored three touchdowns and for the second year in a row, led the team in receptions, with 41.

Muncie, although hobbled by an ankle injury for three games, set a new Saints rushing record with 811 yards, including two 100-yard games. He also caught 21 passes and had seven scores, just short of team MVP Henry Childs' record nine touchdowns.

Muncie scored twice in the 24-20 opening-day loss to the Packers, while three weeks later Galbreath added an NFC high

Tony Galbreath (34) blocks as Chuck Muncie (42) carries the ball around left end. Dubbed "Thunder and Lightning" by Coach Hank Stram, Muncie and Galbreath were the Saints' record-breaking backfield tandem from 1976 to 1980.

nine catches during the Saints' hapless 14-0 loss to San Diego. But the duo soon struck together in a thrilling 27-26 Saints win over the Rams in the Superdome. Muncie pounded out 92 yards and Galbreath collected an even 100 and two touchdowns, as the Saints ground troops outlasted Pat Haden's air corps.

The Saints finished the 1977 season at 3-11, and along with the departure of Hank Stram went the concept and nickname of the "Thunder and Lightning" offense. Stram was replaced by Dick Nolan, and into the Saints' offensive arsenal of Archie Manning, Childs, Galbreath and Muncie, Nolan drafted a new weapon, wide receiver Wes Chandler of Florida.

In 1978 Muncie started only 13 games in the new 16-game schedule, but rushed for 575 yards and seven touchdowns, caught 26 passes and surpassed Manning as the Saints all-time leading rusher, with 2,020 yards. His seven touchdowns tied him for the team scoring title with none other than his backfield partner, Galbreath, who also tallied seven six-pointers during the season.

The durable Galbreath started all 16 games, and along with his seven scores, led the Saints in rushing, with 635 yards. For the third consecutive season Galbreath led the team in receptions. He finished second in the NFL, this time with a Saints record 74 receptions.

Galbreath earned a new nickname, "Mr. Everything," when he even attempted a point after touchdown conversion, after kicker Rich Szaro was injured in a 24-16 loss to Cleveland.

During the '78 season, Galbreath and Muncie's 14 touchdowns helped the Saints reach their second-highest scoring total ever, 281 points, and finish with a franchise best 7-9 mark.

But it was in 1979 that Tony Galbreath and Chuck Muncie had the most explosive season of their record-breaking stay in New Orleans.

Muncie bolted out of the gate with a Saints record 161 yards in the 40-34 opening day overtime loss to Atlanta. He scored on two runs, one a career long 69-yard gallop, and even tossed a 40-yard halfback option touchdown pass to Wes Chandler.

The following week in Milwaukee, Galbreath enhanced his "Mr. Everything" persona by kicking two of three field goals and an extra point in relief of injured rookie kicker Russell Erxleben, during the Saints' 28-19 loss to the Packers.

In the ensuing weeks, Galbreath and Muncie peppered their single touchdown performances with spectacular scoring displays as a touchdown battle between "Mr. Everything" and "the Muncie Burner" began. Galbreath rang up two touchdowns in a 30-21 win in San Francisco, and Muncie responded with two of his own the next week, as the Saints beat the Giants, 24-14. Galbreath added two more scores and completed a pass when the Saints drilled Tampa Bay, 42-14. But he could only get one score in edgewise as Muncie roared for 117 yards and a team record-tying three touchdowns in a 31-20 win over the 49ers. Both players scored once in the Saints' 37-6 revenge in Atlanta.

For Saints fans, the Monday night matchup with Oakland in the Dome became the best of times and worst of times.

During the game, Muncie ran for 128 yards and a score, and became the first Saint to break the hallowed 1,000-yard barrier. Meanwhile, Galbreath was conducting a pass-catching demonstration for the national television audience, grabbing seven Manning passes for 106 yards, including two acrobatic, one-handed stabs, one of which he pulled in for a score. "Mr. Everything" also ran for a touchdown, but the Saints watched a 35-14 lead disappear into a shocking 42-35 loss.

The Saints finished 1979 at 8-8, with 370 points scored, both franchise records. As for the Galbreath-Muncie battle, each started 15 games. Muncie caught 40 passes and had his best rushing season, setting two Saints records, with 1,198 yards and 11 touchdowns. He was named Saints MVP and a Pro Bowl starter, where he rushed for two touchdowns, threw for a third, and received the game's MVP award.

Galbreath also had his best rushing season, with 708 yards. He caught 58 passes, scored 10 touchdowns, and thanks to his two field goals and one extra point, he outscored Muncie, 67 to 66.

The following season, 1980, the Saints finished 1-15. Early into the disastrous campaign, Muncie was traded to San Diego to finish out his career. Galbreath started only four games, but scored two of his season's five touchdowns in the Saints' only win, 21-20, over the Jets. After the season, Galbreath was traded to Minnesota; he finished out his career with the 1985 Super Bowl Giants.

SuperManning

1978 - 1979

In 1978 and '79, Archie Manning started every game for the Saints, and his resulting performances landed him in the Pro Bowl each season.

"Huck Finn in shoulder pads" was one famous description of the '78 Manning, who, as NFC Player of the Year, led Dick Nolan's first Saints team to a franchise best 7-9 record. Manning passed for more than 3,400 yards and 17 touchdowns; his 344 yards during a 20-14 loss to eventual Super Bowl champion Pittsburgh was the NFL season high. He also led the league in completion percentage, and the conference in lowest interception percentage, on his way to first-team All-Pro status.

In 1979 Archie passed for more than 3,100 yards and another 15 touchdowns, again making All Pro, as the Saints improved to 8-8. In his best pro performance to date, he set a Saints record with 355 yards passing, including an NFL season

In 1978, with injuries behind him and a talented supporting cast, Archie Manning received the NFC Player of the Year Award. He earned All-Pro status in both 1978 and '79.

high 85-yarder to Wes Chandler, in a 30-21 win in San Francisco.

Archie considered the '78 and '79 Saints the most potent:

"I was really crazy about Dick Nolan and his coaching staff. But I think the thing that got us, or kept us from going farther, and maybe cost Dick his job, is that he was committed to the flex defense. That's a defense that's very disciplined, and it takes time to implement. And for some strange reason, and I think you've got to give Hank Stram a lot of credit for this, our offense was kind of ready to go. We'd drafted Wes Chandler, we made a trade for Ike Harris, we had Henry Childs, and, of course, Hank had drafted Muncie and Galbreath. And we picked up Conrad Dobler in a trade which really solidified our offensive line. So all of a sudden offensively we've got some weapons, and we're scoring points. And the guys are trying to learn the flex, and we're giving up points. So those were probably the best teams though, especially offensively, because I really had great people to throw the ball to and to hand off to."

When the accolades began to pour in, Archie handled them well:

"I don't think I ever lost track of the fact that football is a team game, and individual accomplishments kind of come second. That was instilled in me early.... Those things probably didn't mean as much to me as they would have if we were going to the playoffs. Certainly, I'd be less than truthful if I said it wasn't satisfying to me. Because I'd developed critics, of course, through the years, and overcome injuries, and people that said I couldn't play. But, as I said before, I had good offensive people.... In many cases, I had good things said and written about me and received some nice honors because of what they did."

In 1980 people were expecting great things from Dick Nolan's Saints, and Archie Manning delivered the best statistical season of his career. But the Saints finished 1-15, after an 0-12 start brought down the curtain on Dick Nolan's reign.

In the year of the "Baghead," Archie played every game and led the NFC in both completions and yardage, throwing for 3,716 yards and 23 touchdowns, both career and team highs. Archie passed for more than 300 yards six times and broke the Saints single-game passing record he set the previous season, with 377 yards and three touchdowns in a 38-35 overtime loss in San Francisco.

But despite his statistical bonanza, Manning considers 1980 his most frustrating season. He recalls:

"We were expected to do well, picked to win our division. We had the same people back. We just got off to a bad start. We lost some close games. At that point, I just don't think overall that the character of our football team was great. We just weren't able to dig down and break out of the thing. And then when we lost so many games where you weren't going to come out of it and get into the playoffs, it just went all the way down. That was very tough, very frustrating. It's no fun losing, but especially when you're losing every week, and when people had expected more. We knew our coach was gonna be fired, and a lot of people (players) know when that happens that they're gonna be gone. And having new players, and starting all over again... So that was definitely the longest year I've spent in football."

In 1981 Bum Phillips took over as head coach, and although injuries sidelined Manning for four games, the Saints improved their record to 4-12.

When he was healthy, Manning led the Saints to their biggest win of the season, 27-24 over Bum's former team, the Oilers.

But during the 1982 pre-season, Bum signed free agent Ken Stabler, his old Houston quarterback, and the writing was on the wall for Manning. After attempting only seven passes in the opening day loss to St. Louis, Archie was traded to Houston for Leon Gray, an offensive tackle who then spent two uneventful seasons in New Orleans.

Archie left the Saints as their all-time leading passer, with his 21,000-plus yards and 115 touchdown passes almost tripling Bill Kilmer's second-place totals. During his career in New Orleans, Archie also ran for over 2,000 yards and 18 more touchdowns, while undergoing seven operations and playing for seven different head coaches and 13 different offensive coordinators.

After leaving New Orleans, Archie labored for two years in Houston, before being traded to Minnesota following the 1983 season. In August of 1985, slowed by the cumulative effects of 14 NFL campaigns, Archie Manning retired from professional football.

Following his fabled college career at Ole Miss, Archie Manning was voted the Southeast Conference's "Quarterback of the Quarter Century." In 1971 his stunning pro debut on a burning September afternoon in Tulane Stadium seemed only to justify the legend -- and enhance the magical aura surrounding the big redhead from Drew, Mississippi.

Looking back on his pro career, Archie has these thoughts:

"Well, I think getting to come in and to play right away may not have been the best thing for me, or for a young quarterback. But I did it, and those highlights you have as a rookie, people seem to make big deals out of. But it was some fun.

"Just to be a quarterback in the National Football League, there aren't but 28 of them, and to be one of them when it was an aspiration you had as a child, it was a big thrill. It was a great accomplishment for me. And the upset wins that we had, and going on in the '78 and '79 seasons to win more games, and also some nice honors to come my way, and to get to play in some Pro Bowl games.

"Now, when I reflect on all those things, they mean a lot more. That I got to do that. And maybe because of that, I don't look back on my career maybe like some people do, as just being one big disappointment and one big, long battle. I look on it favorably. I got to play for 14 years, and I was a starting quarterback for 13 of those years. I made a lot of friends and got to do a lot of things because of it, and I enjoyed the whole trip."

When he retired in 1985, a reporter asked Archie how he'd like to be remembered, and Archie replied, "As a nice guy." He continued:

"My Dad told me that one time when I was going away to college. My Dad just never put that pressure on me. He was very proud of me, but he said, 'I don't care if you become a great quarterback, and you don't have to be an A+ honor student either, but I just want you to do your best in school and in sports, and above all be a nice guy. And so I tried to do that, and I think along the way maybe I got some other honors, some humanitarian things, some things from civic endeavors that maybe said, 'Yeah, he's trying to be a nice guy,' or 'He is a nice guy.' And that always made me feel good."

'Big Ben'

November 12 & 26, 1978

In 1978, utilizing the firepower inherited from Hank Stram, new head coach Dick Nolan was leading the Saints to the best record in team history, behind the explosive talents of quarterback Archie Manning.

The Saints started the season off with a 31-24 upset over perennial power Minnesota, on the shoulders of Tommy Myers' 97-yard return of an errant Fran Tarkenton pass. Later, the Saints evened their record at 4-4, when they stopped the unbeaten division champion Rams, 10-3. It was their first ever victory in the L.A. Coliseum and the Rams' first home loss in 13 games.

New Orleans was 5-5 as they entered a crucial three-game stretch which included two games with their feuding Southern cousins, the 6-4 Atlanta Falcons. Neither New Orleans nor Atlanta had ever qualified for post-season play, but due to the newly created "wild card" playoff spot, the upcoming contests between the two old rivals would be for more than just bragging rights.

In the first clash, before a Superdome record 70,323 fans,

Manning led the Saints to a 17-3 halftime lead. But on the final play before the half, the Falcons unveiled a newly installed play. It was called "Big Ben Right," and it sent several Falcon receivers deep downfield bunched tightly together. Atlanta quarterback Steve Bartkowski then lobbed the ball into the mass of players and hoped for a tipped reception or an interference penalty. The play failed, but was an ominous preview of things to come.

The second half belonged to Atlanta, who fought back and trailed 17-13 with the ball on their 43 yard line and time for just one more play. Bartkowski called "Big Ben Right," and this time it worked. Falcon wide receiver Wallace Francis tipped Bartkowski's bomb at the Saints 15 yard line, and Alfred Jackson grabbed the rebound and carried it into the end zone to defeat the Saints, 20-17.

Saints fans couldn't believe their eyes. They had waited five years to displace the memory of 1973's 62-7 opening day massacre, only to have it replaced by an even more painful event.

Two weeks later in Atlanta, the rematch became a nightmarish flashback. With time running out, and the Falcons once again trailing 17-13, Bartkowski launched another bomb toward the clump of players. This time his last-second prayer was answered with an interference call against the Saints, which set up a one-yard touchdown pass on the game's final play, for another 20-17 verdict.

The Saints finished out of the running at 7-9. But Atlanta's 9-7 record, with six last-minute victories, including four 20-17 wins in the final 10 seconds, earned them the wild card playoff spot.

The Falcons Strike Again

September 2, 1979

The instant the final gun sounded to end the second of Atlanta's 1978 final-play victories over the Saints, New Orleans football fans began counting the days to the rematch.

Now the 62-7 opening-day loss in 1973, which for five years had been an open wound in the psyche of Saints fans, had been replaced by an even more bitter pill to swallow, a pill called "Big Ben." The Saints/Falcons feud was at an all-time high, and the animosity Saints supporters felt toward the Atlanta team was readily apparent when local New Orleans radio personality Eric Tracy introduced the hottest item in town, a T-shirt proudly emblazoned with the phrase, "I hate the Falcons." Not since New Orleans entered the league in 1967 had fan interest been so high in the months preceding the regular season kickoff. And it hit a fever pitch when the 1979 schedule was unveiled, and the hated Falcons were slated to visit the Superdome on opening day.

Nearly 71,000 fans, the largest crowd in Superdome history, turned out to see the Saints administer swift justice to the insolent Falcons. Along with the countless thousands watching the blackout-lifted telecast at home, the fans witnessed a brutal slugfest, with both teams repeatedly giving their best shots.

In the air, Saints Archie Manning and Wes Chandler hooked up six times for a record 205 yards, while Atlanta's Steve Bartkowski hit for three touchdown passes of his own. On the ground, Chuck Muncie rambled for a Saints record 158 yards, while Falcon rookie William Andrews piled up 167 yards and a score. The teams combined for a record 58 first downs, as the game ended regulation time tied at 34.

The Dome was wound tight as a drum as the Falcons won the toss and received the opening kickoff in overtime. But the Saints immediately got the ball back when Tommy Myers intercepted a Bartkowski pass and returned it to the Falcon 46. From there, the Saints couldn't move and the teams proceeded to exchange four punts. With half of the 15-minute overtime period elapsed, the Saints were forced to punt from their 34 yard line. Rookie punter Russell Erxleben finally chased down center John Watson's wild snap at the Saints' one. With Falcons swarming over him, Erxleben tried to shovel a two-handed pass to avoid the safety. The ball was picked out of the air by Atlanta's James Mayberry, who roared into the Saints end zone to abruptly end the game at 40-34.

Erxleben, the Saints' number one draft choice, was hurt on the play and sat out the remainder of the season, but the Saints/Falcons feud was alive and well.

Twelve weeks later, on a rain-soaked field in Atlanta, Manning passed the Saints to a 37-6 win, but it did little to ease the sting of the dramatic opening-day loss.

Saints' mascot "Gumbo," a Saint Bernard, watches the hot and heavy action between his team and those darn Falcons.

Snakebit

December 3, 1979

The 1979 season, which began with a heartbreaking 40-34 overtime loss to Atlanta, was turning out to be the most successful in Saints' history. After an 0-3 start, the Saints had peeled off seven wins in their next 10 games, climaxing with a 37-6 pasting of the Falcons. This victory ran the Saints' record to 7-6 and kept them in a first place tie with the Rams in the NFC's Western Division title race.

As they entered week 14 and a Monday night matchup with the Oakland Raiders, the Saints were smelling playoffs, and head coach Dick Nolan had the players to get them there. The previous season, Nolan had used the wealth of talent left by departing coach Hank Stram to finish with a franchise best 7-9 record. In 1979, five Saints were headed for the Pro Bowl: quarterback Archie Manning, running back Chuck Muncie, tight end Henry Childs, wide receiver Wes Chandler and defensive back Tom Myers.

But the Saints were swimming in dangerous and uncharted waters. No New Orleans team had ever been realistically in an NFL playoff hunt this late in a season, and Nolan's squad was anxious to prove they were legitimate contenders. But for the Saints, the Monday night proving ground was also traditionally unwelcome territory.

In three appearances on the nationally televised prime time spectacle the Saints were winless. In 1972 they had lost to Kansas City, 20-17, followed the next season by a 40-3 embarrassment in Dallas. In 1974, in their last Monday night episode, the Saints had lost 28-7 to the reigning World Champion Pittsburgh Steelers, who were on the way to their second straight Super Bowl title.

The Saints had waited four long years to be invited back to the Monday night institution, and when the game started, they made the most of their opportunity.

In a loose, fast-flowing contest, the Saints jumped out quickly and led 28-14 at halftime and 35-14 in the third quarter, thanks partly to some spectacular plays by running back Tony Galbreath. But Oakland quarterback Ken "Snake" Stabler brought the Raiders roaring back with two late touchdown passes to Cliff Branch, one a 66-yard bomb to tie the game at 35, and the second, an eight-yarder to beat the Saints, 42-35.

During the game, Muncie became the first Saint to break the 1,000-yard rushing mark, but the loss dimmed the Saints' playoff hopes, and the following week's 35-0 blowout by San Diego finished them off. The Saints ended the season with a team record 8-8 mark, but the Rams, at 9-7, won the division and advanced to a Super Bowl date with the Steelers.

The Saints returned to Monday night football the following year, but that night's 27-7 loss to the Rams prompted Dick Nolan's firing and sparked another two-year Saints absence from the Monday night schedule.

The 'Baghead' Saga

1980

After an 8-8 finish in 1979, the best record in New Orleans franchise history, Saints fans looked to 1980 as the year head coach Dick Nolan would finally bring them a winner. Instead, their hopes crumbled, as Nolan's troops stumbled toward a 1-15 mark, the worst finish in the NFL and the worst in Saints history.

It was after their seventh straight defeat, a 41-14 stomping by the Atlanta Falcons, that New Orleanian Jerry Gogreve walked into Charlie's Saints Marching Club Bar with a shopping bag pulled over his head, playfully hiding both his shame and identity from his fellow mourning Saints fans. Thus began one of the most unique and humorous chapters in the love affair between the Saints and their fans, who for 14 weeks in 1980 became known as "Bagheads."

Another patron at the bar that fateful afternoon was Gogreve's friend Robert LeCompte, who also happened to tend bar at a local lounge owned by popular New Orleans sports-

Bags such as this one were worn over the heads of thousands of wounded Saints fans in the Superdome in the 1980 season, when the team went 1 and 15.

caster Buddy Diliberto. The following day, LeCompte took Gogreve's idea one better. He painted a paper grocery bag gold and black and wrote the word "Aints" across the bottom. He then called Diliberto, who wore the bag during his telecast that night, creating an instant sensation.

Hearing opportunity knocking, LeCompte immediately ordered 5,000 "official" gold and black Aints bags, and within a week had sold 3,000 of them at one dollar a bag.

Bag fever now began spreading like wildfire throughout the Saints faithful, who had finally found the perfect symbol for

14 seasons of frustration and losing. The true diehards would continue to publicly support their heroes on Sundays at the Superdome, but they'd ride out this seemingly endless storm incognito.

Following two more road losses, the Saints returned home to a Superdome filled with "Bagheads." Along with LeCompte's "official" bags, thousands of fans turned out sporting their own personalized versions. Some wore full body bags, while others glued bags together, creating team editions for the whole family to enjoy. There were Christmas bags, complete with lights and trimming and, of course, the basic, one-size-fits-all, brown grocery bag.

The next week the Bagheads hit the road as part of the annual Saints fan migration to Atlanta, and watched through their bag holes as the Saints stretched their winless streak to 11.

By now the "Bagheads" were nationally famous, as the newspaper wire services and network television all jumped on the story of the long-suffering, but good-humored Saints fanatics.

The "Bagheads" continued to multiply as the winless streak hit 12, and Coach Nolan, who three months before held sway over the hopes and dreams of a franchise, was replaced by interim coach Dick Stanfel.

Finally, after 14 consecutive defeats, the Saints, propelled by two Tony Galbreath one-yard touchdown runs, eked out a 21-20 victory over the Jets during a dizzying New York snowstorm, and the bags were mercifully put to rest, thus ending one of the most infamous episodes in Saints history.

But the "Baghead" saga didn't end in New Orleans. Much to the regret of struggling teams everywhere, Saints fans had begun a trend. Today when a team begins losing, "Bagheads" are sure to pop up in the stands until the streak ends. And when the suffering team looks for someone to blame for the bags, they can point their fingers South, to Jerry Gogreve, Robert LeCompte and the 1980 New Orleans Saints, the patron saints of the "Bagheads."

Faith, Hope And 'Bum'

1981 - 1985

In 1981 Saints fans all over Louisiana put bumper stickers on their vehicles that read "Faith, Hope and Bum." O. A. "Bum" Phillips had come to New Orleans after being unexpectedly fired by the Houston Oilers, a team he had taken to within one game of the Super Bowl in two of their previous three seasons.

Once in New Orleans, Bum began the task of rebuilding from the shambles of the Saints' 1980 1-15 disaster by choosing Heisman Trophy running back George Rogers with the first pick in the NFL draft. He added other outstanding selections like future Pro Bowl linebacker Rickey Jackson, quarterback Dave Wilson and fullback Hokie Gajan from LSU.

Led by Rogers' league-leading and NFL all-time rookie rushing record 1,674 yards, the Saints finished 4-12 in 1981.

The season was highlighted by a first-ever two-game sweep of the Rams and a 27-24 grudge match victory over Bum's former team, the Oilers.

The '82 season began with another strong draft, bringing offensive lineman Brad Edelman and place-kicker Morten Andersen to town. But, in the first and perhaps most controversial of Bum's many controversial trades, starting quarterback and local institution Archie Manning was sent to Houston for tackle Leon Gray after one week of the regular season, thus clearing the deck for Bum's former Oiler quarterback, Ken "Snake" Stabler.

Behind the crafty Stabler and Rogers' second straight All Pro season, the Saints finished 4-5, and in this strike-shortened season they narrowly missed the playoffs.

In 1983, Bum's third season in charge brought the Saints to the brink of the playoffs, but a game-winning Rams field goal with six seconds left in the season's finale, kept the 8-8 Saints home for the holidays once again.

Before the '84 draft, Bum traded the Saints number one pick to the Jets for quarterback Richard Todd, and six games into the schedule, he sent the Saints' first-round choice in 1985 to the Oilers for his old warhorse running back Earl Campbell.

Two games later, "Snake" Stabler retired on the Monday following a 30-27 overtime loss to the Cowboys. The overtime had been forced when Stabler, replacing an injured Todd, fumbled while being sacked in his end zone, and Dallas recovered for a touchdown.

The Saints finished 1984 at 7-9, and before the '85 season could begin, Phillips dealt George Rogers, the Saints' all-time leading rusher, to Washington for their number one pick. The Saints got off to a 3-2 start in 1985, but then fell into a six-game losing streak as Bum's former magic vanished.

Finally, in week 12, the Saints defeated Minnesota, 30-23. The following day Bum Phillips, with a Saints career mark of 27 wins and 42 defeats, resigned as the winningest head coach in New Orleans Saints history.

Saints head coach Bum Phillips scratches his head as he wonders what he needs to do to get his team winning consistently.

'King George'

1981 - 1984

In 1981 George Rogers blasted from the South Carolina campus to the Saints--and then directly into the record books with the most prolific rookie season by a running back in NFL history.

Bum Phillips had drafted Rogers hoping to build his offense around the speedy but punishing Heisman Trophy winner. In week two Rogers shattered the first of nine Saints records that he would leave in the wake of his spectacular rookie campaign. He ripped the Rams for a record 162 yards and a score, as the Saints won, 23-17. But it was against Philadelphia, one month later in the Superdome, that Rogers first showed Saints fans his explosiveness, taking off on a team record 73-yard non-scoring run, and finishing with 134 yards and two TDs. The following week, in a 20-17 loss at Cleveland he gained 122 yards and broke loose for a Saints record 79-yard touchdown run. Three games later, "King George," as he was now being called, popped off a 59-yarder, while plowing through the Rams for 161 yards and a team record-tying three

George Rogers used his slashing running style to become NFL Rookie of the Year in 1981, setting an NFL rookie rushing record with 1,674 yards.

touchdowns.

Rogers added five other 100-yard days and finished the season with an all-time NFL rookie rushing record, 1,674 yards. His yardage, 13 touchdowns, and nine 100-yard games were all Saints records, and earned him NFL Rookie of the Year and All Pro honors.

A hamstring injury in 1982 sidelined Rogers for three of the strike season's nine contests. Still, he finished All Pro, with 535 yards and three touchdowns, including 166 yards and a score in Dallas, for the NFL's top rushing performance.

Opening day 1983 saw a healthy George Rogers return to his record-breaking form with 206 yards and two touchdowns, one a game-breaking 76-yarder, in a 28-17 win over St. Louis. The following week versus the Rams, Rogers was once again on a fast clip, gaining 42 yards in the first quarter, before torn knee ligaments sidelined him for three games. He returned for three 100-yard days and finished the season with 1,144 yards and five touchdowns.

In 1984 Rogers began with 102 yards and two touchdowns in a 36-28 opening day loss to Atlanta. But it would be the last time Rogers surpassed the 100-yard mark or scored a Saints touchdown. He finished the season as the Saints' leading rusher with 914 yards. But before the 1985 season began, apparently due to the emergence of Hokie Gajan and the arrival of Earl Campbell, Rogers was traded to Washington for a number one draft choice, which the Saints used to pick linebacker Alvin Toles.

George Rogers left New Orleans as the Saints all-time leading rusher, having gained 4,267 yards and scoring 23 touchdowns during his four-year reign.

Heartbreaker

December 18, 1983

The Saints' 1983 season was down to do-or-die as they faced the Los Angeles Rams in the final week of the schedule. The situation for Bum Phillips' third Saints season windup was simple: Both teams were 7-9, the winner would get a wild card playoff spot, the loser would get a ticket home and an off-season haunted by "what ifs."

But Bum had had his fill of "what ifs." After a 4-12 mark in 1981, he had brought the Saints in at 4-5 for the strike-shortened 1982 season, only to miss the playoffs in a complicated tie-breaking system. In 1983 the playoffs seemed attainable, but the season had been an emotional roller coaster ride that had taken its toll on both the team and their fans.

It started opening day in the Superdome with George Rogers' team record 206 yards rushing against St. Louis. Then a three-point loss to the Rams preceded the Saints' first-ever overtime win, a 34-31 thriller over Chicago in the Dome. It continued in week four with a teeth-clenching 21-20 loss to the Cowboys after a last-second sack of Saints quarterback Kenny Stabler.

Other losses were offset with nail-biting wins, like a two-pointer over Atlanta and a three-pointer over Tampa Bay. But the last four nerve-racking weeks before the Rams finale had been brutal.

First there was a fist-pounding, 31-28 Monday night loss to the Jets on a last-second punt return, then a white-knuckle 17-16 Saints victory over Minnesota. Next, was a helpless 7-0 loss to the Patriots in a blinding New England snow storm, followed by another overtime ulcer-inducer, a 20-17 win at Philadelphia.

The 70,000 Saints faithful who packed the Dome for the Rams showdown, surely thought they had felt it all, but they didn't realize that the Saints' roller coaster had yet to reach its highest and, unfortunately, lowest points.

The game was seesaw, with the Rams scoring in odd ways, including a safety on a sack of Kenny Stabler and touchdown returns of both a punt and an interception. But the Saints, behind backup quarterback Dave Wilson, still managed to lead 24-23 with only minutes to go. Then Bum Phillips made perhaps his most crucial and controversial decision as Saints head coach. He decided not to let Morten Andersen try a 49-yard field goal, even though Andersen had kicked 50- and 52-yarders the previous week, outdoors in Philadelphia.

The Rams got the ball back, drove 55 yards in eight plays, and with six seconds left rookie Mike Lansford kicked a 42-yard field goal to win the game, 26-24.

The Saints roller coaster finally crashed to Earth, as the Rams went to the playoffs and Saints fans filed out of the Superdome in stunned silence.

After a respectable 7-9 finish in 1984, Bum Phillips resigned 12 weeks and four wins into the 1985 season, seemingly unable to shake the stigma of the 1983 heartbreaker.

Hokie

1981 - 1987

Hokie Gajan was special. A tenth-round Saints draft choice in 1981, he somehow managed to hang on despite early freak injuries, and by 1984 the barrelling fullback had quietly become the Saints' main offensive threat.

Hokie, whose full name is Howard Lee Gajan Jr., was a Baton Rouge native and a four-year letterman at LSU. He spent 1981 on the Saints' injured reserve list, the result of an auto accident that left him with a gash on his forehead. Hokie cemented his inactive status for the season when he broke his ankle while working out waiting for his forehead to heal.

But his year on the Saints' injured reserve list helped Hokie get comfortable with the Bum Phillips system, and in the strike-shortened 1982 season, Hokie saw action in all nine games, starting four. By 1983 Hokie's determination and hard work began to pay off. He had come to the Saints at 5 foot 11 inches, 205 pounds, but by 1983 he had added a full 25 pounds of muscle to his frame. He possessed the strongest pair of legs on the team, capable of lifting 1,300 pounds on the leg machine, and prompting teammate Ken Stabler to nickname him "The Bayou Bowling Ball."

In 1983 as the Saints headed toward an 8-8 record, tying the franchise best, Hokie began to make his presence known. In week ten he scored two touchdowns, including the clincher, in a 27-10 must-win over the Falcons in the Superdome. But it was two weeks later, with the Saints record at a precarious 6-5, before a crowd of 68,000 in the Superdome, that Hokie gave a Monday night national television audience a glimpse of what he could do. Hokie rambled for 113 yards, oddly the only 100-yard-plus effort of his career, including a 58-yard trip that set up George Rogers' short touchdown run for a 28-14 Saints lead. However, the New York Jets mounted a furious comeback, capped by a 76-yard punt return for a touchdown and a 31-28 victory.

Hokie started 12 games at fullback in 1983, finishing third in rushing behind Rogers and Wayne Wilson and leading the team with 5.1 average yards per rush. But his flashes of brilliance in 1983 were only a hint of what was to come the following season.

In 1984 Hokie Gajan became the Saints' most powerful and dependable weapon. He started 14 games and led all NFL starting backs with a team record 6.0 yards per carry. He led the team in receptions, was second only to George Rogers in rushing, and didn't fumble once all season. He also led the Saints with seven touchdowns, and even threw a touchdown pass himself.

Hokie's individual game exploits were numerous. In week two the Saints trailed Tampa Bay 13-10 with less than two minutes to play, when Hokie took quarterback Richard Todd's swing pass and rolled 51 yards with it down to the Buccaneer 13 yard line. Two plays later he tallied the winning score from eight yards out for a 17-13 win. Week four saw Hokie throw a 34-yard touchdown pass to Wayne Wilson in a 34-24 Saints win over St. Louis in the Superdome. The following week the

Hokie Gajan gets ready to throw a TD pass to backfield mate Wayne Wilson during the Saints' 34-24 win over St. Louis in 1984. Gajan was an ex-LSU hero who hung on with the Saints and became their most potent and reliable offensive weapon before injuries shortened his promising career.

Saints' defense recorded their best effort in history, holding the Houston Oilers to only 133 total yards while the Gajan machine continued to hit on all cylinders, and the Saints record improved to 3-2. Hokie led the Saints with 90 yards on the ground, and two scores, including a late 37-yarder that sealed a 27-10 New Orleans victory over Bum's former team in the Astrodome.

In week eight the Saints blew a 27-6 lead and suffered a frustrating 30-27 overtime loss in Dallas, leading to Ken Stabler's retirement from football the following day. Hokie however, shone in defeat, once again leading all Saints ball-carriers and highlighting his performance with a career-long 62-yard touchdown run.

The next week Hokie led all Saints receivers with six catches, led all Saints rushers with 52 yards, and scored the only Saints touchdown in a crucial 16-14 victory over the Browns.

As the season wound to a close, Hokie missed two games, but returned in week 14 to lead Saints rushers for two straight weeks. In the final game of the season, a 10-3 win over the Giants in New York, Hokie again scored the game's only touchdown, and the Saints finished perhaps the most frustrating season in their history at 7-9.

As the 1985 season approached, it was obvious that Hokie Gajan's star had officially risen. He had proven himself beyond any shadow of a doubt during the grueling '84 season, and after Bum Phillips traded leading rusher George Rogers to Washington on April 26 everyone knew that Hokie would be expected to carry the lion's share of the Saints' ground game in the upcoming campaign.

Hokie responded as expected, leading the Saints in rushing the first three games of the season. But in week four, after scoring his second touchdown of the new season during a 20-17 win in San Francisco, Hokie pulled a hamstring muscle, thus beginning his slow descent into retirement. He would carry the ball only seven more times for the Saints, and although he fought courageously to come back, his brilliant career flickered and eventually faded away.

Two weeks after the hamstring injury, Hokie tried to return during a loss to the Raiders in Los Angeles, but three carries were enough to send him back to recovery. One month later, in week ten, Hokie returned to the Saints' starting lineup for the final time against the Seattle Seahawks in the Superdome. On his first three carries, Hokie was magnificent, rushing for 26 yards during the Saints' opening drive. But on his fourth carry, Hokie was hit at the Seattle two yard line and injured ligaments in his knee. The injury required surgery and sidelined him for the remainder of the '85 season and all of the 1986 season, effectively ending his career.

It was a time of change for the Saints. The following week Bobby Hebert, a native Louisianian and a refugee from the defunct USFL, would make his first NFL start at quarterback for the Saints. Two weeks later Bum Phillips would retire, opening the door for the hiring of another USFL alumni, head coach Jim Mora, and the beginning of a new era in Saints' history.

Hokie Gajan would never play another regular season down for the New Orleans Saints. After an attempt to regain his old form during the 1987 training camp, Hokie injured his other knee and retired from professional football on August 17, 1987, becoming a player personnel scout for the Saints.

No Mora Excuses

1986

Following the 1985 season, his first as team owner, Tom Benson was determined to make the Saints a winner. First he hired Jim Finks as president and general manager, followed by Jim Mora as head coach.

Mora had won 48 of 62 USFL games, leading the Philadelphia/Baltimore Stars into each of the league's three title games. In 1983 they lost the championship to Bobby Hebert's Michigan Panthers, but won it in 1984. In '85 they defeated Hebert's Oakland Invaders for their second USFL title.

Mora was a hard-working, no-nonsense coach who stressed defense and ball control, and knew how to get it. From the USFL he signed linebackers Vaughan Johnson and Sam Mills and running back Buford Jordan. From the college draft, running backs Dalton Hilliard and Rueben Mayes and linebacker Pat Swilling fit the Mora mold perfectly.

In week two of Mora's inaugural NFL campaign, quarterback Bobby Hebert hit two bombs, of 76 and 84 yards, and the Saints defense added a team record seven interceptions to defeat Green Bay, 24-10. The next week, in a 26-17 loss at San Francisco, USFL

Jim Mora took over as head coach of the Saints in 1986 after becoming the winningest coach in the USFL, with a 48-13-1 record. "I like this challenge," said a confident Mora. "Taking over a team that is looking for its first winning season appeals to me."

graduate Mel Gray returned a kickoff 101 yards for a score, but a broken foot sidelined Hebert for the next 12 games. In week four, after quarterback Dave Wilson's 63-yard touchdown pass to Eric Martin, the Saints blew a 17-0 halftime lead over the eventual Super Bowl champion Giants and lost, 20-17. Week seven saw Mora's defense add five sacks and three forced fumble recoveries to Rueben Mayes' two touchdowns in a 38-7 win over Tampa Bay.

In the rematch with San Francisco, the defense held the 49ers to 52 yards rushing, while the fast-emerging Mayes added two more scores in a 23-10 Saints victory. The following week the Saints defense blocked a crucial Rams field goal and held NFC rushing champ Eric Dickerson to 57 yards, as two Morten Andersen field goals spelled a 6-0 Saints shutout for New Orleans.

Later in the season, the tough New Orleans defenders held New England to just two yards rushing during a 21-20 loss. Against Miami, Mayes rambled for 203 yards and two more scores, but the Saints again came up short, 31-27.

The defense was led by linebacker Rickey Jackson's 117 tackles, nine sacks and six forced fumbles. In week 15 in Atlanta, Jackson dominated the Falcons with 12 solo tackles and four sacks, one on the game's final play, to preserve a 14-9 Saints win.

Mora's first Saints team finished 7-9, while Mayes ended with 1,353 yards, six 100-yard games, eight touchdowns and the NFL Rookie of the Year award. He joined Jackson and Morten Andersen in the Pro Bowl.

Johnny Comes Marching Home

1987

As Saints head coach Jim Mora prepared his team for the 1987 season, his second at the helm, there loomed a large storm cloud on the horizon. For the second time in a decade, the NFL Players Association was threatening to cancel the NFL season by calling a general players' strike. Five years earlier they had used the same means to cancel nearly half of the NFL's 16-game schedule, shortening the season to a total of only nine games. Now, in 1987, another strike seemed certain, but this time the NFL owners were ready.

Anticipating the strike, coaches had kept tabs on players released during training camp and pre-season, and when the Players Association officially called the strike after the second weekend of regular-season games, the owners and coaches needed only one week off to organize "replacement" teams

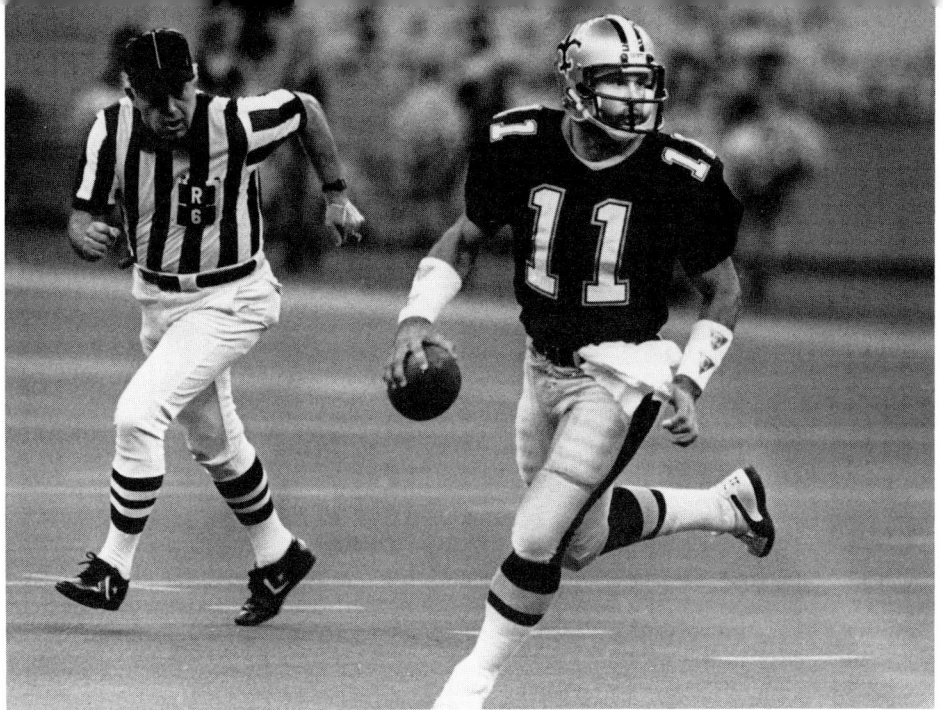

New Orleans native John Fourcade prepares to throw one of three touchdowns in his first NFL start, leading the Saints' replacement team to a 37-17 win over the Rams during the 1987 players' strike.

before continuing on with the regular schedule.

Once the strike was called, Mora and the Saints coaching staff went right to work, contacting released players and free agents to add to the handful of veteran players who would refuse to honor the strike. Most of the players they contacted jumped at the chance to put on a helmet once again, leaving their various civilian jobs in an instant for another shot at the NFL. Running back Dwight Beverly, who would become the Saints' leading rusher during the three replacement games, was working as a nightclub bouncer in Canada when he got the call to come to New Orleans. Offensive tackle Ken Kaplan was a part-time UPS worker and a full-time student who became an instant Saint, as did linebacker Joe DeForest, who left his post as a logistics engineer at Kennedy Space Center in Florida. Both started all three replacement games for the Saints.

But to secure the services of the most famous and prolific of their replacement players, the Saints didn't even have to make a long-distance phone call. Quarterback John Fourcade, a native New Orleanian, was working as a teacher and football coach at a New Orleans high school. When the strike hit, several teams contacted Fourcade. He was reportedly on his way to the airport and the Los Angeles Raiders when the Saints called. The chance to quarterback the hometown Saints in front of the fans who had watched his football career soar and eventually flutter was too much to pass up.

Most New Orleanians had given up hope of ever seeing John Fourcade in the NFL, scratching their heads in wonderment as the hometown hero went from the "can't miss" list to the "whatever happened to..." file. In high school Fourcade had quarterbacked the Shaw Eagles to the city crown, establishing himself as a cocky leader and a top college prospect. He signed with Ole Miss and in four seasons used his freewheeling style to rewrite the Rebels' record book, breaking practically all of former Ole Miss legend Archie Manning's passing records. By the end of his senior season, Fourcade was all-everything and in January of 1982 he was named the South's MVP in the Senior Bowl. He returned home and waited for the upcoming draft and his entry into the NFL ranks.

But a funny thing happened on draft day: John Fourcade's phone didn't ring. The draft came and went with all 28 NFL teams passing on Fourcade.

Different people had different ideas to explain why such an outstanding collegian would be ignored on draft day. Some said it was his size, 5-11, 205 pounds, or the collarbone surgery he had following the Senior Bowl. Others said that the phrase "cannon for an arm, loose cannon for a mouth" pretty much summed him up.

But Fourcade had his own opinion. During the 1981 season, ex-Ole Miss head coach Johnny Vaught (who had called the shots during the glorious Manning era), remarked that if he were still the Rebels' coach, Fourcade's lack of discipline would have kept him out of the lineup. Also, just a few days prior to the draft, a Toronto newspaper quoted Fourcade as saying that he'd go to the Canadian Football League if he wasn't drafted in the "first two rounds." Fourcade argued that he said he'd go to Canada if he wasn't chosen in the "first two days" of the draft.

Regardless, Fourcade seems to have concluded that Vaught's comments plus the newspaper article contributed heavily toward his not being drafted into the NFL, thus setting him off on a long, rocky road.

"Some people thought I was playing the CFL off the NFL, looking for more money. Money has never figured into my thinking. People said I was cocky. Said I had a big mouth, that I was arrogant. I might have said some things that I shouldn't have said. Hey, I was a football player wanting to play football. But I wasn't a renegade, " Fourcade says.

Fourcade did want to play football, and over the next five years he proved it. Following the draft debacle, eight NFL teams wanted Fourcade to sign as a free agent, but instead he opted for the CFL's British Columbia Lions and the beginning of a journey that would make stops in four different cities and three different leagues. The USFL began play in 1983, and Fourcade returned to the States to join up with the Birmingham Stallions. In 1984 he called signals for the USFL's Memphis Showboats, and he returned there in '85 for the league's final season.

In 1986 Fourcade returned home and tried to catch on with the Saints as a free agent, but first-year head coach Jim Mora was unimpressed and Fourcade was cut without much fanfare or opportunity. It could have easily been the end of the line, and for a while even Fourcade thought it was.

"I thought about quitting. I actually gave up on playing football. I thought, 'Maybe they're right. Maybe I'm not good enough to play.' I just wanted to get on with my life," Fourcade recalls.

He returned to Ole Miss to complete his degree, but in May of 1987 he decided to give pro football what he thought was his last shot, signing with the CFL's Toronto Argonauts. Five days later he was released and returned home. But then another new league, this one playing on a 50-yard field and called the Arena Football League, beckoned, and Fourcade became a quarterback with the Denver Dynamites during their stretch drive to the first Arena Bowl championship. In August he accepted a teaching position at John Ehret High School in suburban New Orleans, and began watching with a vested interest as the NFL headed toward an inevitable strike. When the Saints called, he said "yes."

"Thank God for the strike. When the strike hit, about eight clubs called. In the back of their minds, I think people knew I could play, but they were afraid to take that chance with me. All I ever wanted was a chance, but nobody gave me a chance. I just thank Jim Finks and Jim Mora for giving me that opportunity," he says.

The Saints took the chance with Fourcade, and although he was only one of many players who got an opportunity to show his talent with the advent of the strike, few, if any, seized the moment in such spectacular fashion as the former Ole Miss Rebel.

After the cancellation of week three's games, the NFL resumed play on Sunday October 4 with the replacement teams, and a curious crowd of 29,745 came to the Superdome to watch the Saints tee it up against the Los Angeles Rams. All week long conversations had revolved around whether or not Fourcade, after all of his travels, would still have what it took in his NFL debut. It didn't take long for the hometown fans to get their answer. In the first quarter Fourcade took the Saints on a methodical, time-consuming, 17-play drive, ending it with his first NFL touchdown pass and a 7-0 Saints lead. The second quarter got off quickly when Saints first-year defensive back Reggie Sutton blocked a Rams punt, picked it up and scored, increasing the margin to 13-0. Fourcade followed with his second touchdown pass, an 11-yarder to Eric Martin, one of 14 Saints veterans who would eventually cross the strikers' picket lines to play in the replacement games. Later in the quarter, Fourcade engineered another long drive, this one a 12-play set that ended in the Rams end zone and a 27-0 Saints lead. In the fourth quarter, leading 30-3, Fourcade put the icing on his NFL debut, hooking up with tight end Mike Waters on an 82-yard touchdown, setting a record for the longest scoring pass in Saints history, and sealing a 37-10 victory.

After years as a journeyman, travelling through three different leagues and four different cities, John Fourcade's courageous play during the 1987 players' strike earned him a home on an NFL roster, with the Saints. He felt most at home in the end zone.

In his first NFL start Fourcade was impressive, directing the Saints to 14 of 18 third down conversions and completing 16 of 21 passes for 222 yards and three touchdowns. By the time the final gun sounded, John Fourcade was a hero. His five-year journey through rival leagues and foreign cities had ended, appropriately, in his hometown. But the job wasn't over.

The following week the new Saints travelled to St. Louis and Fourcade picked up right where he had left off against the Rams, directing the Saints offense on a 14-play drive in the opening series. But when the drive stalled, a Saints field goal attempt turned into a Cardinal touchdown when Saints holder, and backup quarterback, Kevin Ingram fumbled the snap and a Cardinal returned the ball for a touchdown. Trailing 10-0 in the second quarter, Fourcade injured his knee and was replaced by Ingram, who again fumbled, this time while attempting to pass. The fumble was once again scooped up and returned for a St. Louis touchdown, and the Saints trailed 17-0. Fourcade returned to action in the second half and furiously led the Saints back, aided by running back Dwight Beverly's 139 yards rushing and two touchdowns. But late in the fourth quarter, with Fourcade leading the Saints to the apparent winning score, Beverly fumbled to end the Saints final legitimate scoring opportunity, assuring a 24-19 Cardinal victory.

On the Thursday following the second weekend of replacement games, with a growing number of players crossing the picket lines and negotiations going badly, the Players' Association announced the strike was over, and the striking players agreed to return to their teams following the third replacement weekend. For the overwhelming majority of replacement players it meant that they had one game left in their brief NFL careers. But for John Fourcade, it meant he had one game left to win a spot on the team's regular roster, and he had waited too long to let this opportunity slip through his fingertips.

Things started badly for the Saints in their final replacement game in Chicago. The Bears, the NFL's only remaining unbeaten team, turned a Saints fumble and a Fourcade interception into a 10-3 lead, before Reggie Sutton blocked a Bears punt and the Saints recovered it for an apparent touchdown. But Sutton was called for holding and the Bears maintained possession and drove to a 17-3 lead. With the contest threatening to get out of hand, and the remainder of his prime NFL opportunity ticking away with the game clock, Fourcade buckled down and once again led a Saints comeback, hitting Eric Martin with a 14-yard touchdown pass to close the gap to 17-10 at halftime. In the second half Fourcade and the Saints controlled the ball, driving to three more Florian Kempf field goals and a 19-17 lead. The defense did the rest, shutting the Bears out, with Reggie Sutton intercepting his third pass of the day to stop the final Chicago drive and seal the Saints second replacement victory.

Fourcade passed for 198 yards and a touchdown, and the obvious question on everyone's mind was, "Will Fourcade be retained by the Saints?" He was. Fourcade's field leadership, courageous play and versatility had earned him a spot on the Saints' regular roster. The 2-1 record of the replacements contributed to the overall 12-3 mark that set a team record for wins and earned the Saints their first playoff appearance in franchise history.

Following the win over the Bears, the Saints veterans returned to work and regained their positions. But when the bulk of replacement players returned to civilian life, John Fourcade remained a Saint.

For most players the replacement games had been an unrealistic final stab at NFL glory, but for a few it was a legitimate second chance at NFL life. By the beginning of the 1988 season four replacement players (Fourcade, Mike Waters, wide receiver Stacey Dawsey and nose tackle Pat Swoopes) were still on the Saints roster. Seven more had impressed Saints coaches enough to be invited to training camp as free agents. But only one, John Fourcade, had managed to capture the imagination of his hometown and turn his second chance into the NFL career that had so long eluded him.

The Promised Land

1987

Through 20 long years of suffering, the Saints had remained the only team in the NFL without a winning season or a post-season playoff appearance. Both the team and its fans had endured two decades of hollow "wait until next year" boasts that never came true. But 1987 was looking different.

As the Saints headed into game 12, they were riding a five-game win streak, the longest in team history. Finally, the Saints had all the horses: A coaching staff led by eventual NFL Coach of The Year Jim Mora, a consistent offense, a suffocating defense, and a big-play kicking team that led New Orleans to an 8-3 record. With only four games remaining, due to the strike-shortened schedule, the Saints were already assured of

Two decades of waiting for "next year" finally ended on December 6, 1987, when the Saints defeated Tampa Bay 44-34, clinching their first NFL playoff berth. The fans believed the team could do it, and the support they showed was instrumental in this and other victories.

their first winning season. But they wanted more. The Saints wanted a playoff berth, and to once and for all throw off their tag as the only NFL team to have never made the playoffs.

The Saints opponent in week 12 was the Tampa Bay Buccaneers. The Buccaneers were the only team in the NFL that the Saints could actually claim a winning record against, having won six of their nine contests.

Once the game started the Saints wasted no time jumping on Tampa Bay quarterback Vinny Testaverde. The Heisman Trophy winner, making his first pro start, fumbled on the Bucs' first two possessions, leading to two quick Bobby Hebert-to-John Tice touchdown strikes, and the Saints were off and running, 14-0.

The Saints led 28-10 at the half after Rueben Mayes and Dalton Hilliard both scored on short runs. Then Mayes added

Saints owner Tom Benson celebrates on the field as the team makes the playoffs for the first time in their history, with a victory over Tampa Bay.

another short touchdown run early in the third quarter to put New Orleans up 38-10. Punt returner Mel Gray set up both of Mayes' TDs with a record-setting 80-yard return and a 50-yard return.

Buccaneer rookie Testaverde had an impressive debut, throwing for two second half touchdowns while trying to keep Tampa Bay close. But the Saints used Bobby Hebert's personal high of 255 yards passing and three second half field goals from Morten Andersen to stay comfortably ahead and win, 44-34.

That was it. With this win, the Saints had finally clinched the first playoff berth in franchise history. Crowds filled the French Quarter in celebration, as endless choruses of "When the Saints Go Marching In" echoed through the streets until the wee hours.

Twenty years of frustration and waiting were over. The Saints had finally reached the promised land, the playoffs.

Epilogue

In 1987 the New Orleans Saints erased 20 seasons of dashed hopes, faded dreams and unrealized potential during one glorious 12-3 campaign, finally shedding their mantle as the only NFL team never to have had a winning season. Head Coach Jim Mora had used his USFL blueprint of ball-control offense and game-control defense to lay a solid foundation upon which he would build future successes.

Over the next few seasons, the suffocating defense, anchored by a Pro-Bowl linebacking corps known as the "Dome Patrol," made up of Rickey Jackson, Sam Mills, Vaughan Johnson and Pat Swilling, and the offense, led by the home-grown "Cajun Cannon," Bobby Hebert, and other Louisiana men like running back Dalton Hilliard and wide receiver Eric Martin, both ex-LSU stars, combined to execute Mora's philosophy to near perfection.

As the 1988 season opener approached, the Saints had an impressive winning season under their belts as they prepared to shelve the memory of the "Aints" forever and take the next step toward becoming one of the NFL's most respected franchises.

Additional copies of
The New Orleans Saints (Book 1)
and
The New Orleans Saints (Book 2)
(Publication date : March 1992)

can be ordered from : Acadian House Publishing, P.O. Box 52247, Dept. SB1, Lafayette, LA 70505, Phone (318) 235-8851

To order, send $14.85 per book (That's $11.95 for the book, $2.00 for shipping and 90 cents for tax) to the address above. (Non-Louisiana residents deduct 90 cents tax.) Be sure to specify on your check or in a note which book(s) you are ordering and how many.

◆

Want to learn more about Louisiana's intriguing culture, heritage and history?

Much of what you may want to know can be found in the pages of *Acadiana Profile,* "The Magazine of the Cajun Country," and in the books published by Acadian House Publishing, including these:

- *Louisiana's French Heritage*
- *The Truth About the Cajuns*
- *Cajun Cooking* Cookbooks (A set of 2)
- *Cajun Country Tour Guide & Festival Guide*
- *The Character of the Cajun Country* (A pictorial)
- *Live Oak Gardens: A Place Of Peace & Beauty*
- *The Treasures of Avery Island*

For a free brochure, write to the address above.